*Cover Picture:*
*Crystal Palace, 7 October 1857.*

C.H. Spurgeon is best-remembered today for the remarkable ministry he exercised in London during the Victorian era. His influence was incalculable. Thousands listened to his preaching every week, while hundreds of thousands throughout the world later read his sermons in published form.

A man of great natural gifts, charm and wit, Spurgeon's master passion was evident in everything he did – to preach Jesus Christ to all as the only Saviour. But as early as 1855 this brought him into a serious and prolonged doctrinal controversy with Hyper-Calvinism.

By tracing this conflict, exploring the issues involved in it and showing what was at stake in them, Iain H. Murray underlines the contemporary relevance and importance of sharing C. H. Spurgeon's convictions.

# Spurgeon *v.*
## HYPER-CALVINISM

# SPURGEON *v.* HYPER-CALVINISM

## The Battle for Gospel Preaching

### Iain H. Murray

NEW PARK STREET CHAPEL

## THE BANNER OF TRUTH TRUST

THE BANNER OF TRUTH TRUST
3 Murrayfield Road, Edinburgh EH12 6EL
P.O. Box 621, Carlisle, Pennsylvania 17013, USA

\*

© Banner of Truth Trust 1995
First Published 1995
Reprinted 1997
Reprinted 2000
Reprinted 2002
ISBN 0 85151 692 0

\*

Typeset in 12/13pt Bulmer MT'
at the Banner of Truth Trust, Edinburgh
Printed in Finland by WS Bookwell

# ABBREVIATIONS

*NPSP*     *New Park Street Pulpit* (London: Passmore and Alabaster), Spurgeon's sermons and annual volumes for 1855–1860.

*MTP*     *Metropolitan Tabernacle Pulpit* (London: Passmore and Alabaster). This series succeeded the six volumes of the *New Park Street Pulpit*. The first volume of *MTP*, with sermons for the year 1861, was therefore numbered volume seven. Annual publication continued until 1917.

*ST*     *The Sword and the Trowel* (London: Passmore and Alabaster), ed. C. H. Spurgeon, published monthly from January 1865 and in annual volumes.

# Contents

## PART 3
## ILLUSTRATIVE MATERIAL

# *Preface*

After a break of some thirty years I am very glad in these
pages to be able to write something more on Charles
Haddon Spurgeon. In November 1961 I was asked to
speak on Spurgeon in Sheffield. Out of that address
grew some articles in the *Banner of Truth* and finally *The
Forgotten Spurgeon* (1966). The present book came about
in a similar way. In May 1995 I was invited to give an
address on 'Spurgeon's Battle with Hyper-Calvinism' at
the Grace Baptist Assembly in London. In preparing for
that occasion I soon found that there was more useful
material than could possibly be used in one address and
these pages are the result.

The two books deal with two quite different controversies although they are not altogether unrelated.
Arminianism – the main theme of *The Forgotten Spurgeon*
– sets aside the scriptural teaching of the sovereignty of
God in salvation. All men are equally condemned in sin
but, for reasons unknown to us and to the praise of his
grace, God does not deal equally with those who are
equally undeserving. The testimony of Scripture ought to
be unmistakable: 'as many as were ordained to eternal life
believed' (*Acts* 13:48). But does the denial of Arminianism
mean that God has no love for all? that Christ is not to be
proclaimed as the Saviour in whom all are called to trust?
Does the particularity of grace mean that there can be no
universal entreaties, no gospel for 'every creature'? Hyper-

Calvinism answers 'Yes' to these questions and in so doing it constitutes a serious hindrance to the progress of the evangel.

It is a cause for thankfulness that even as a young man Spurgeon could both oppose Arminian thinking and be a resolute opponent of Hyper-Calvinism. Robert Shindler, who knew him from 1855, could affirm in 1892: 'Mr Spurgeon, with all his strong attachment to truths which relate to divine sovereignty – and he has ever been bold and unflinching in his proclamation of them – has always presented the other side, the call of the gospel to all who hear it.'[1] In an important comment in the *Sword and the Trowel,* Shindler, himself a pastor among the Baptists from 1850, wrote of the effect of Spurgeon's stand for *evangelical* Calvinistic preaching from the mid-1850s as he had observed it. Shindler's own congregation was at that date on the Hyper-Calvinistic side until Spurgeon came to New Park Street:

'By means of the circulation of his sermons, taking people to hear him, when he preached in the neighbourhood, and getting him to preach for me, a very powerful influence was brought to bear upon my congregation, and on others outside of it. So it came to pass that, in very many circles of Baptists, ministers and others, the truth of the universal call of the gospel to sinners as sinners was accepted as an integral part of the gospel; and when it was not accepted, it was to some extent tolerated.

'That part of Mr Spurgeon's work has scarcely been

---

[1] R. Shindler, *From the Usher's Desk to the Tabernacle Pulpit, The Life and Labours of Pastor C. H. Spurgeon* (London: Passmore and Alabaster, 1892), p. 36.

noticed by his biographers; but it was immensely important, and has been the means of untold blessing. I remember the first sermon he preached in my chapel; it was from the text, "All that the Father giveth Me shall come to Me; and him that cometh to Me I will in no wise cast out." I can see the smiles that played over the faces of many, whose theology began and ended in the blessed declarations of Romans viii. Alas, how all was changed when he came to the latter part of the text! The honey was turned to gall, and the smiles gave place to scowls.

'Our beloved brother and leader's testimony, in these later years, though essentially the same, has had widely different aims. It was not that the scope of gospel teaching might be widened, but that the gospel itself might be retained in the pulpits of his and other denominations.'[1]

Shindler's comment on how the times had changed between the 1850s and the Down-Grade controversy of the 1880s is a reminder of how danger does not always come from the same quarter. As a Puritan once said, 'The devil does not allow the wind of error to blow long in the same direction.' In the 1960s it seemed to many of us that Spurgeon's continuing significance had to do with his witness to the free-grace convictions of the Reformers and Puritans over against the shallow and non-doctrinal evangelicalism of our day. Thirty years later that witness remains relevant and yet it is apparent that the recovery of doctrinal Christianity is not necessarily our chief need today. In many churches there has been a real increase in knowledge and a resurgence of Calvinistic belief has occurred across the world. The word 'forgotten' is happily

---

[1] 'Mr Spurgeon's Early and Later Ministry', *ST*, 1892, p. 420.

far less applicable to Spurgeon than it was forty years ago. But it may well be that the time has come when we need to be much more familiar with a rather different emphasis in Spurgeon.

While I know of no evidence that Hyper-Calvinism is recovering strength, it would appear that the priority which soul-winning had in Spurgeon's ministry is not commonly *seen* to be our priority. The revival of doctrine has scarcely been matched by a revival of evangelism. While not accepting the tenets of Hyper-Calvinism it may well be that we have not been sufficiently alert to the danger of allowing a supposed consistency in doctrine to override the biblical priority of zeal for Christ and the souls of men. Doctrine without usefulness is no prize. As Spurgeon says, 'You may look down with contempt on some who do not know so much as you, and yet they may have twice your holiness and be doing more service to God.'[1]

The danger with Hyper-Calvinism is not so much what it believes, but that it does not believe enough. By bringing that to light in the controversy of the 1850s Spurgeon has left a vital testimony and one as 'immensely important' now as it was then.

On the subject of this book, there is only one point known to me at which Spurgeon's later thought showed a variation with his early years. He very largely abandoned the practice of calling other Christians 'Hyper-Calvinists' or 'Arminians'. The terms may not be intended to be derogatory, yet in controversy they soon begin to carry that sense and thus may alienate the fellow Christians to whom they are applied. In his maturer years he indeed came to

[1] *MTP*, vol. 11, p. 34.

use all 'labels' more sparingly, not because his mind was changed on the errors in question, but rather because the best way to help others is simply to teach the Scriptures. Love of the truth which is not accompanied by love for others brings no honour to God and love will show itself, in part, in the words we use or decline to use. Even so, there is a system of thought which has to be recognised as Hyper-Calvinism and in the interests of clarity the term is often unavoidable.

I am indebted to many for their help in various ways: to Robert Oliver for the diagram he has kindly supplied for use in these pages and for advice generously given; to Daphne Pierce for bringing my attention to the little-known cameo picture of Spurgeon written by Mrs Curtis; to Elizabeth Catherwood and John R. de Witt for kindly reading the proofs; to Jack Houghton and the Evangelical Library, London, for their aid with sources; to Doreen Adams for all her enthusiasm in carrying forward the actual production of this book; and, not least, to my wife, without whom not only this book but so much else could never have been done.

I count it as one of the great blessings of my life that I had a set of Spurgeon's *Metropolitan Tabernacle Pulpit,* and the desire to read them, when I was young. My hope and prayer is that many young ministers today will learn the life-long habit of reading Spurgeon. A pastor's wife told me recently, 'Spurgeon has been with us ever since our honeymoon.' May the number of such happy households be increased!

Iain H. Murray
August 1995

# PART ONE

# *An Introduction to Spurgeon*

'The lamp of my study – C. H. Spurgeon, 1856.
'The light is as bright as ever – 1861.
'Oh, that mine eyes were more opened! – 1864.
'Being worn to pieces, rebound 1870. The lantern mended, and the light as joyous to mine eyes as ever.'

Words in Spurgeon's Bible.

'We marvel more and more at the abiding novelty and power of the Word. The clear flowing stream of Scripture may well sing –

> *Men may come, and men may go,*
> *But I go on for ever;*

Ever living, ever fresh, ever refreshing, fertilizing, life-giving, the river of God, which is full of water, sparkles in the sunlight of heaven as brightly now as it did a thousand years ago, and is as brimming with holy floods of consolation, as when first it made glad the city of God.'

*Metropolitan Tabernacle Pulpit,* vol. 10, p. v.

'It is our ambition to be great believers, rather than great thinkers; to be child-like in faith ... What the Lord has spoken he is able to make good; and none of his words shall fall to the ground.'

*Metropolitan Tabernacle Pulpit,* vol. 36, p. 304.

# 1

## *A Life of Testimony to the Word of God*

In a sermon he once preached on 'Trembling at the Word of the Lord', Spurgeon illustrated a point he was making by an incident in the life of the famous French preacher, Jean Baptiste Massillon. After Massillon had preached on a certain occasion one of his hearers was heard to exclaim, 'What an eloquent sermon! How gloriously he preached!' When the words were reported to Massillon he replied, 'Then he did not understand me. Another sermon has been thrown away!' We may say the same in regard to Spurgeon. Simply to praise Spurgeon is to miss something far more important. The real reason why he ought to be remembered today is an altogether higher one. In the light of the passing of centuries and the brevity of human life, even the greatest of men in themselves are only shadows. 'Our lives', said Spurgeon, 'are but like seconds in the tide of this great time of ours, which is itself but a second in the great duration of eternity.'[1] Or as Winston Churchill once confessed in sorrow, 'We are only specks of dust, that have settled in the night on the map of the world.'[2] The one thing which ultimately gives significance to any man is his

[1] *MTP,* vol. 60, pp. 547–8.

[2] Martin Gilbert, *Road to Victory: Winston S. Churchill, 1941–45* (London: William Heinemann, 1986), p. 581.

relationship to God, and how he will finally stand before the judgment seat of Jesus Christ. For us to speak about the dead is in a sense to anticipate that judgment and that might be entirely improper were it not that we already know the standard by which the deeds and words of all men will be measured, 'the word that I have spoken, the same shall judge him in the last day' (*John* 12:48). The relationship of Charles Haddon Spurgeon to the Holy Scriptures is therefore our starting point in these pages.

### The Bible and Understanding History
To make Scripture our starting point has added significance by reason of the times in which we live. The religious scene is one of confusion and uncertainty. Churches and denominations are commonly regarded as having lost a clear sense of direction. Their one-time influence in the nation has been largely lost and no one is sure how it is to be recovered. A few years ago an article by a religious correspondent in *The Times* attributed these conditions 'to muddled leadership and uncertainties of purpose in every church'.[1] Although he died over a hundred years ago, we believe Spurgeon anticipated our present situation. He believed that a change of such a fundamental character was taking place in the church of the last century that its results would be felt generations later. The popular view among church leaders of the Victorian era was that Protestant Christianity would go 'full steam ahead' in the twentieth century. Spurgeon said the opposite. He found himself like Jeremiah, warning that the promises being made by his

---

[1] 'The Decade of Evangelism was never going to work', *The Times*, 18 January 1992.

religious contemporaries were false. He knew there were sad days ahead: 'We are only at the beginning of an era of mingled unbelief and fanaticism. The hurricane is coming. Men have ceased to be guided by the word, and claim to be themselves prophets.'[1]

The above quotation goes to the root of the difference between Spurgeon and so many of his religious contemporaries. Victorian Christianity fell to the old temptation of putting confidence in human understanding and trust in man's abilities. Certainly the century had seen a vast increase in knowledge. In the realm of science new discoveries had taken place with astonishing rapidity. A century that began with oil lamps and horse-drawn transport was ending with electricity and express trains. It seemed feasible to argue that even the Bible had to be affected by such an explosion of new understanding. It was said that the educated could no longer accept the idea of a Book which is authoritative in all that it says, and so the majority of Christian leaders retreated to what they believed was a more defensible position, namely, the view that the Bible is only *partially* inspired of God. All the denominations quietly made allowance for this new view of Scripture. At the same time it was claimed confidently that this change would have no effect upon the essential message of the Bible, for Christianity, it was said, means trusting in Christ, not in a book. It is the living experience of Christ that matters, not arguments or theories about Scripture. Such statements were to be heard both from men who boasted of 'modern thought' and from those who claimed to remain evangelicals. Evangelical experience, the

[1] *MTP*, vol. 29, p. 214.

latter asserted, remained unaffected by a man's view of Scripture.[1]

In contrast with such views, Spurgeon held that to allow a partial acceptance of Scripture would be fatal to the cause of real Christianity. His reasons were these:

1.    An acceptance of the new view changes a man's whole relation to the Bible. It no longer puts men *under* Scripture but makes them the assessors of what is or is not to be received: 'The new religion practically sets "thought" above revelation, and constitutes man the supreme judge of what ought to be true.'[2] The reader of Scripture ceases to be the humble sinner and becomes the critic. 'If it is left to me to discriminate and to judge how much of this Book is true, and how much false, then I must myself become infallible or what guide have I?'[3]

Further, once this approach is accepted then, as Spurgeon saw, everything becomes open to doubt: 'If we doubt God's Word about one thing, we shall have small confidence in it upon another thing. Sincere faith in God must treat all God's Word alike; for the faith which accepts one word of God and rejects another is evidently not faith in God, but faith in our own judgment, faith in our own taste.'[4]

If the Bible is only partially inspired then no doctrine can be received simply on the grounds that it is the teaching

[1] See, for example, the case of Robertson Smith in *The Life of Alexander Whyte*, G. F. Barbour (London: Hodder & Stoughton, 1923), p. 217, or of T. R. Glover in *Evangelicalism in England,* E. J. Poole-Connor (London: Fellowship of Independent Evangelical Churches, 1951), pp. 249–51.

[2] *ST,* 1888, p. 43.

[3] *MTP,* vol. 36, pp. 9–10.    [4] *MTP,* vol. 36, p. 303.

of Scripture. What this would mean in the final outcome was that 'salvation' is not to be related to any set of beliefs at all. 'I change my creed every week', a minister once told Spurgeon, supposing that his lack of fixed beliefs had nothing to do with the genuineness of his Christianity. In contrast with such a position, Spurgeon preached: 'Let us hold fast, tenaciously, doggedly, with a death grip, to the truth of the inspiration of God's Word ... Everything in the railway service depends upon the accuracy of the signals: when these are wrong, life will be sacrificed. On the road to heaven we need unerring signals, or the catastrophe will be far more terrible.'[1]

2.    Spurgeon believed that this new attitude to Scripture was not, in fact, what it professed to be. It professed to be the result of intellectual honesty, an acceptance of the fact that Christian belief had to be adjusted to new knowledge. It claimed that where the traditional view of Scripture was preserved it could only be by men of narrow, closed minds who were blind to progress. If the church was going to advance then she would have to accommodate her testimony to modern knowledge. This sounded plausible but it was ignoring one great fact: disagreement with Scripture was not a nineteenth-century phenomenon. In the first century it was written, 'the world by wisdom knew not God' (*1 Cor.* 1:21). It is a fundamental characteristic of fallen

---

[1] *MTP*, vol. 36, p.167. J. C. Ryle speaks equally forcefully against the theory of partial inspiration: 'Once admit the principle that the writers of the Bible could make mistakes ... I see nothing certain, nothing solid, nothing trustworthy in the foundations of my faith. A fog has descended on the Book of God and enveloped every chapter in uncertainty.' *Expository Thoughts on John,* vol. 3 (1873; repr. Banner of Truth, 1987), pp. viii–ix.

human nature that the carnal mind is enmity against God and therefore at enmity to the truth which God reveals. Ever since the Fall man has wanted to alter, to weaken, to disbelieve, the Word of God. That is the explanation for the way in which men disbelieved the testimony of Jesus Christ, the incarnate Word. To his learned Jewish hearers Jesus said: 'Why do ye not understand my speech? even because ye cannot hear my word ... He that is of God heareth God's words: ye therefore hear them not, because ye are not of God' ( *John* 8:43, 47).

Spurgeon saw that behind the debate over such questions as the authorship of particular books of the Bible lay an opposition to Scripture which arose from the hostility of the unregenerate mind. 'The only real argument against the Bible is an unholy life. When a man argues against the Word of God, follow him home and see if you can discover the reason of his enmity to the Word of the Lord. It lies in some form of sin.'[1] What led men to propose the toleration of a partial acceptance of Scripture was not the advance of real knowledge, it was compromise with unbelief. The church was being tempted to suppose it could retain the essence of Christianity while escaping from the offence which scriptural truth gives to the world.

---

[1] *MTP*, vol. 35, p. 618. This is not, however, to say that Spurgeon regarded all who abandoned faith in the infallibility of Scripture as non-Christians. It was rather a principal part of his sorrow in the Down-Grade controversy that Christians *were* being deceived for they were being carried along by a current popularised by worldly men. For the Down-Grade controversy, see my *Forgotten Spurgeon* (Banner of Truth, revised edition 1973). Much on Spurgeon's convictions on Scripture will be found in *ST* for 1887–89.

3. Above all, Spurgeon held that this was no mere debate about words and opinions. At the heart of Scripture lies the assertion that God's attitude to men is vitally related to their attitude to his Word. According to Scripture, faithfulness to God and faithfulness to Christ are synonymous with faithfulness to their *words*. There is no such thing as reverence for God, or loyalty to Christ, without obedience and faith in their words (*Matt.* 7:24–6; *Matt.* 28:20; *John* 8:31; *John* 14:23, etc.). Spurgeon is only repeating what Scripture itself says when he writes: 'Unless we receive Christ's words, we cannot receive Christ; and unless we receive the apostles' words, we do not receive Christ; for John saith, "He that knoweth God heareth us; he that knoweth not God heareth not us. Hereby know we the spirit of truth and the spirit of error."'[1]

It was from this axiom that Spurgeon could prophesy with certainty that the course of the churches of the twentieth century would be very different from that which the popular teachers imagined. If God promises to look with favour only upon those who tremble at his word (*Isa.* 66:2), then the Christianity which fails at that point is sure to lack the anointing and authority of the Spirit of truth. This knowledge was the great burden of Spurgeon's later years. On the basis of what was being so widely accepted, he saw the catastrophe which lay ahead. 'Modern theology if it were put in the Garden of Eden would not see a flower. It is like the sirocco that blasts and burns, it is without either dew or unction; it proves itself to be unblest of God and unblessing to men.'[2]

[1] *An All-Round Ministry,* (1900; repr. Banner of Truth, 1960), p. 373.
[2] *MTP,* vol. 39, p. 266.

**Spurgeon's Life in Summary**

A brief summary of Spurgeon's life may help to set his
thought in context. After a childhood in Essex, when he
owed much to Christian parents and grandparents, he
was converted in 1850 at the age of fifteen. He was then
assisting at a school in Cambridge and it was in these
Cambridge years that he came to Baptist principles and
was called to the Baptist pastorate in the near-by village of
Waterbeach. From there he moved to New Park Street,
London in 1854 at the age of nineteen.

Roughly speaking his public work can be divided up
into four decades. Through the 1850s he was 'The Youthful Prodigy' who seemed to have stepped full-grown into
the pulpit. At the age of twenty the largest halls in London
were filled to hear him; at twenty-one the newspapers
spoke of him as 'incomparably the most popular preacher
of the day'; when he was twenty-three, 23,654 people
heard him at a service in the Crystal Palace. In the next
decade, the 1860s, his work might best be described in
terms of 'The Advancement of Gospel Agencies'. The in-
stitutions which he founded, and for which he remained
responsible, included a College to train pastors; a publications enterprise (with a weekly published sermon and a
monthly magazine); an Orphanage; a Colportage Association to spread Christian literature; and above all the
Metropolitan Tabernacle itself, opened for the church he
served in 1861 and capable of holding about 6,000. The
congregation which he pastored grew from 314 in 1854 to
5,311 in 1892.[1]

---

[1] The progression was as follows: (1859) 1,332; (1864) 2,937;
(1869) 4,047; (1875) 4,813. Spurgeon rarely made any allusion to
these numbers and often warned of 'counting heads'.

Onlookers often supposed that so many enterprises could never be maintained at the high level of usefulness with which they began, but they were, and the 1870s might well be described in terms of 'Holding the Ground'. On every front the work was being blessed. Then came the 1880s and by far the most difficult period in Spurgeon's life. In this last decade he was faced with increasing controversy and a title for his last years could well be his own words, 'In Opposition to So Many'.[1] By the time Spurgeon was fifty-seven in 1891 his health was utterly broken. When he left Herne Hill station, London, on 26 October 1891, for the south of France, he said to the friends who came to say good-bye, 'The fight is killing me'. He died at Menton three months later. Hearing the news in South Africa, one of his former students wrote in his College notebook, 'Dear CHS Passed into the Heavens'.[2]

### The Bible as the Explanation for Spurgeon's Work

Spurgeon's ministry was even more remarkable than the few facts recorded above would indicate. If we take into account both his spoken and written word, it is estimated that each week his 'congregation' amounted to about a million people. By 1899 it is on record that 'over an hundred millions' of his sermons had been issued in twenty-three languages.[3] These sermons, published weekly from 1855, were also put out in bound, annual volumes, making up a

[1] *An All-Round Ministry*, p. 395.

[2] Rev. John Russell whose four MS notebooks of his years at Spurgeon's College remain in South Africa today.

[3] *C. H. Spurgeon's Autobiography* (London: Passmore and Alabaster, 1899), vol. 2, p. 73.

series of 63 volumes, the last of which appeared in 1917 – a quarter-of-a-century after his death! In addition to all this, Spurgeon published about 150 other works and edited 28 volumes of *The Sword and the Trowel*. Passmore and Alabaster, his publishers, made history in their ability to prosper while virtually confining themselves to the writings of one single author. Writing three years after Spurgeon's death, William Williams could say: 'The productions of no other preacher's heart and brain ever kept a great printing and publishing firm constantly engaged with the issue of his works alone. I have been through the publisher's store rooms; these contain many *tons* of Mr Spurgeon's works, which are in constant demand.'[1] Williams then goes on to quote sales figures.

The obvious question is, how could any man retain such influence over so many people through such a long period? How can we account for the enduring interest? How could a man speak so often, and write so much, without losing his freshness and his appeal? It is true Spurgeon possessed unusual gifts, and that he worked very hard, but we cannot get anywhere near the real answer if we think merely in terms of what he was or did. The explanation lies in the Book that was in his hands, the Book that was his constant companion, and which he lived to preach and study. All the blessing he attributed to that source. His own thoughts, his own opinions, would have achieved nothing:

'"The law of the Lord is perfect, converting the soul"; nothing else but the living Word of God will convince, convert, renew and sanctify. He has promised that this shall

---

[1] William Williams, *Personal Reminiscences of Charles Haddon Spurgeon* (London: Religious Tract Society, 1895), p. 287.

not return unto Him void; but He has made no such promise to the wisdom of men, or the excellency of human speech. The Spirit of God works with the Word of God ... All his paths drop fatness; but man's paths are barrenness.'[1]

In possessing the Bible Spurgeon believed that the church has an inexhaustible source of light and heat. What he said once of John Bunyan could be equally said of himself, 'Prick him anywhere and his blood is bibline'. The content of his sermons and his books is plain, you might say, ordinary, Scripture. The energy of his prayerful adherence to Scripture is the true explanation of his work:

'The Bible is a wonderful book ... You can use it for a lamp at night. You can use it for a screen by day. It is a universal Book; it is the Book of books, and has furnished material for mountains of books; it is made of what I call *bibline,* or the essence of books ... This one Book is enough to last a man throughout the whole of his life, however diligently he may study it.'[2]

### The Bible and the Content of Spurgeon's Faith

One of the deepest convictions of Spurgeon's life was that there is a continuity in the work of God and that continuity centres round the body of truth which lies in Scripture, 'the faith which was once delivered unto the saints'. He believed that at the Protestant Reformation God had restored that body of truth and that it had been summarised in masterly form in the creeds and catechisms of the Reformers and Puritans. This deposit of saving truth has to be passed on faithfully from one generation to another. The

[1] Address on 'Beaten Oil for the Light', *ST,* 1892, p. 687.
[2] *MTP,* vol. 28, p. 190.

nineteenth-century obsession with originality he regarded as a sin when it was found among the professed custodians of the Word of God.[1] For him the apostle's command was still binding, 'the things that thou hast heard of me among many witnesses, the same commit thou to faithful men, who shall be able to teach others also' (*2 Tim.* 2:2).

In 1855 Spurgeon reprinted the 1689 Baptist Confession of Faith – the Confession which belongs to the same family as the Westminster Confession – and when the Metropolitan Tabernacle was being built in 1859 he had a copy placed under the foundation stone. Instead of adopting the diluted creeds which marked the last century he held the deposit of doctrine that arose out of the Reformation as a heritage of biblical truth to be preserved and handed on to coming generations. For the same reason he had the children and young people of his congregation taught the Shorter Catechism of 1647, revised only on the point of baptism. Referring to this fact, he said in 1866: 'The fashion is to laugh at this book, and to say it is out of date, and so on. Well, I should like to see someone write a better summary of scripture doctrine.'[2] Similarly, he did not hesitate to tell members that if they did not believe

---

[1] 'Don't worry about originality, brethren; Christ never claimed it. He says: "The words that I speak are not Mine, but His that sent Me". The Holy Spirit did not claim it, for it is written, "He shall not speak of himself, but whatsoever He shall hear, that shall He speak".' Williams, *Personal Reminiscences,* p. 140.

[2] *Speeches of C. H. Spurgeon* (London: Passmore and Alabaster, 1878), p. 64. 'Our children who have learned "the Westminster Assembly's Confession of Faith", know more about the doctrines of grace and the Bible than hundreds of grown-up people who attend a ministry which very eloquently teaches nothing.' *MTP*, vol. 12, p. 430.

doctrines explicit in the Confession of Faith they could not remain members 'with a clear conscience'.[1]

This emphasis in Spurgeon's ministry had very important consequences. For one thing, it meant that Spurgeon's fundamental sympathies and commitment could be easily recognized as identical with historic evangelical Christianity. He was a definite Baptist but his allegiance to evangelicalism took precedence over the things which aligned him with Baptists. His whole ministry demonstrated a biblical catholicity. The men he put at the head of the Pastors' College and the Orphanage were both paedo-baptists.[2] One of the two partners in the publishing firm to which he gave his total support was an Anglican. In the Down-Grade controversy of his later years, Spurgeon regarded it as a tragedy that Baptists put their denominational unity before a higher claim. Preaching on 'Our Expectation' about the time of that controversy, he said: 'Christian people, you ought to have a clannish feeling! "Oh", says one, "you mean that the Baptists ought to get together!" I do not mean anything of the kind. I mean that the seed of Christ should be of one heart; and we ought to recognize that, wherever the life and love of Jesus Christ are to be found, there our love goes out.'[3]

---

[1] *Only A Prayer-Meeting* (London: Passmore and Alabaster, 1901), p. 67.

[2] *C. H. Spurgeon Autobiography*, vol. 2, *The Full Harvest* (revised edition of original *Autobiography*, Banner of Truth, 1973), p. 168. Volume 1, *The Early Years*, was published in 1962. To avoid confusion with the original *Autobiography*, these two revised volumes will be cited below as *C. H. Spurgeon: The Early Years* and *C. H. Spurgeon: The Full Harvest*.

[3] *MTP*, vol. 37, p. 55.

Another consequence of the priority which Spurgeon gave to the fundamentals of the faith was that, while his work inspired the study of Scripture itself, at the same time it also introduced his hearers and readers to a great succession of teachers and expositors who belonged to one common school of faith. It would scarcely be too much to say that Spurgeon's sixty-three volumes of sermons are but a condensation of the wealth of evangelical writing already existing in the English language. One day in his study he pointed a friend to shelves loaded with the works of English Puritans and said, 'I have preached them all'.[1] He had preached more besides but it was chiefly drawn from that same tradition. The result is that anyone who gives himself to reading Spurgeon will not be fed on a diet of nineteenth-century theological fashions, he will not be entertained with short-lived theories that were merely the quirk of a great individual, he will rather be given a love for a body of truth which has a past and a future – truths which will outlive all the oddities, errors and fantasies that arise to distract the church from her true calling.

There were plenty of would-be teachers in the last century who, in order to establish their own supposed discoveries, claimed that 'the teaching of the Holy Spirit' had delivered them from all need of 'dead men's brains'. They found in Spurgeon a resolute opponent. In the authors they affected to despise he saw a gift of Christ to the churches of all ages.[2] The supposed superiority of the latest voices to teachers of the past was but another form of human pride.

[1] Williams, *Personal Reminiscences,* p. 34.

[2] See Spurgeon, *Commenting and Commentaries* (1876; repr. Banner of Truth, 1969), pp. 26–7.

## The Bible and Spurgeon's Personal Life

The Scriptures clearly teach that there is a definite connection between what men are in private and their public usefulness. That part of our lives which is least seen by others is the part which has the controlling influence upon what we are and what we do. In every true Christian leader, therefore, the part of his life least known to the world will always be that which is the most important.

Prior to his conversion at the age of fifteen, Spurgeon was for four years under conviction of sin, conscious of his inability to meet the demands of the ten commandments. It was in this painful experience that the foundation of his dependence on the Word of God was first laid. 'God's law had laid hold upon me ... Before I thought upon my soul's salvation, I dreamed that my sins were few.'[1] The responsibility for the length of this period of conviction has been laid by some on the injurious influence of Puritan books. That is certainly not how Spurgeon saw it. 'I wondered why I experienced so many spiritual conflicts while others were in peace. Ah, brethren, I did not know that I was destined to preach to this great congregation. I did not understand in those days that I should have to minister to hundreds, and even thousands, of distressed spirits, storm-tossed and ready to perish.'[2]

Spurgeon's personal conflicts by no means ended with

[1] *C. H. Spurgeon: The Early Years*, pp. 58-9.
[2] *MTP*, vol. 29, pp. 213-4. In 1890 he was to say: 'We have few Puritans because we have few penitents. An awful sense of guilt, an overwhelming conviction of sin, may be the foundation stone for a gloriously holy character' (*MTP*, vol. 38, p. 56).

his conversion. Had they done so, he came to see, he would have been ruined. Fallen men, though Christians, cannot long be surrounded by popularity and success without the special help of God. 'Our God takes care always to have security that, if he works a great work by us, we shall not appropriate the glory of it to ourselves. He brings us down lower and lower in our own esteem ... Some trumpets are so stuffed with self that God cannot blow through them.'[1] 'You may rest quite certain that, if God honours any man in public, he takes him aside privately, and flogs him well, otherwise he would get elevated and proud, and God will not have that.'[2] 'Many a man has been elevated until his brain has grown dizzy, and he has fallen to his destruction. He who is to be made to stand securely in a high place has need to be put through sharp affliction. More men are destroyed by prosperity and success than by affliction and apparent failure.'[3]

These statements were very much part of Spurgeon's own personal experience. They go far to explain much of the fruitfulness of his ministry and its close attachment to Scripture. Not until after his death was it more generally known what great personal trials he had to pass through. His much-loved wife, Susie, was a semi-invalid throughout the greater part of his ministry. In 1867, when Spurgeon

---

[1] *Only A Prayer-Meeting*, p. 42.    [2] *MTP*, vol. 52, p. 165.
[3] *MTP*, vol. 51, p. 356. Elsewhere he says: 'There is tinder enough in the saint who is nearest to heaven to kindle another hell if God should permit a spark to fall upon it. In the best of men, there is an infernal and well-nigh infinite depth of depravity. Some Christians never seem to find this out. I almost wish they might not do so, for it is a very painful discovery for anyone to make: but it has the beneficial effect of making us cease trusting in ourselves' (*MTP*, vol. 52, p. 225).

was only thirty-three, his own health began to break down in a bout of severe illness. Two years later he had a first attack of what was then known as gout, a disease which causes painful inflammation of the joints of the body. By the year 1871 he had come to think that sudden attacks of this disease would be what he calls 'our cross till death'.[1] That proved to be correct. The disease took its usual course, spreading slowly from the feet upwards. Sometimes Spurgeon spoke of both feet and a hand as 'a mass of pain'. His condition was generally worse in cold weather and his doctors believed that it was aggravated by excessive mental labour. As well as the physical anguish which attended these bouts, there were experiences which troubled him still more, namely what he calls 'frightful mental depression'.[2] There were dark days when he was prostrated by despondency as well as by illness.

These and other trials Spurgeon came to believe were blessings from God. He could say, 'I have been much the gainer by my sad hours and my sick days'.[3] Or again, 'I believe the affliction was necessary for me and has answered salutary ends'.[4] On their bedroom wall were the words of the text, 'I have chosen thee in the furnace of affliction'. Commenting on what happens in that furnace, he says, 'beauty is marred, fashion is destroyed, strength is

---

[1] *C. H. Spurgeon: The Full Harvest*, p. 194. Recovering from illness in 1871, a poignant letter to his congregation includes the words: 'Nights of watching and days of weeping have been mine, but I hope the cloud is passing. Alas! I can only say this for my own personal and light affliction; there is one who lies nearest my heart whose sorrows are not relieved by such a hope' (*Ibid.*, p. 85).

[2] *Ibid.*, p. 410.          [3] *MTP*, vol. 35, p. 224.

[4] *C. H. Spurgeon: The Full Harvest*, p. 410.

melted, glory is consumed'. It is there that we learn to pray, 'O Lord, sink me in self that I may rise in thee'.[1] In private and solitude Spurgeon was taught that he was nothing before God. He could say: 'I have turned over my sermons, and my many labours for the Lord, but there is scarce one of them that I dare to think of without tears, – they are all marred by sin and imperfection. As I think of every act I have ever done for God, I can only cry, "O, God, forgive the iniquity of my holy things!"'[2]

One of his fullest comments on his repeated illness is to be found in an editorial in the *Sword and the Trowel* in May 1876, 'Laid aside. Why?' in the course of which he wrote:

'Consciousness of self-importance is a hateful delusion, but one into which we fall as naturally as weeds grow on a dunghill. We cannot be used of the Lord but what we also dream of personal greatness, we think ourselves almost indispensable to the church, pillars of the cause, and foundations of the temple of God. We are nothing and nobodies, but that we do not think so is very evident, for as soon as we are put on the shelf we begin anxiously to enquire, "How will the work go on *without me?*" As well might the fly on the coach wheel enquire, "How will the mails be carried *without me?*"'

Behind Spurgeon's usefulness there lay this hidden cost. Repeated trials persuaded him that without help from heaven he would utterly sink under his own weakness, his troubles and his responsibilities. Yet it would be entirely wrong to speak as though chastisement formed the main

---

[1] *The Cheque Book of the Bank of Faith* (London: Passmore and Alabaster, 1888), p. 312. See also *ST,* 1887, p. 110.

[2] *MTP*, vol. 53, p. 329.

part of his private dealings with God. It was only preliminary to something else. God exalts the humble. Spurgeon
entered deeply into the love of Christ and into the comfort
of the Holy Spirit, and it was this which made him the
bright and joyful Christian that he was. On this subject he
often quoted words he had learned in his youth:

> *Though cares like a wild deluge come,*
> *and storms of sorrow fall;*
> *When I have fed with Christ at home,*
> *My soul defies them all.*

But our main concern here is to refer to the means by
which this help came to him and which was then passed on
to others. That means was the Bible. His testimony was
that without the Word he would never have endured. 'The
Holy Spirit', he constantly says, 'acts as Comforter through
the Word.' Spurgeon needed the Scriptures, and loved the
Scriptures, in the first instance, for his own faith and for his
own growth in grace. He was not the professional, studying
the Bible only to teach others, for his personal study of
Scripture went far beyond what was necessary for sermon
preparation. Thus he spent more than twenty years preparing the largest commentary on the Book of Psalms that
has ever been compiled although no duty required him to
do it. No publisher commissioned him. The influence
which kept him at it was the enrichment which came to
him through living so closely with that part of Scripture.
The very title he gave to the commentary indicates what he
felt. He called it, *The Treasury of David*, and when the
work was finally done he testified to 'the wealth of mercy
that has been lavished upon me' from the Psalms. 'Blessed
have been the days spent in meditating, mourning, hoping,

believing, and exulting with David! Can I hope to spend hours more joyous on this side of the golden gate.'[1]

When Spurgeon died he was preparing yet another expository work on Scripture, *The Gospel of the Kingdom, A Popular Exposition of the Gospel According to Matthew.*[2]

Another vital role which Scripture exercised in Spurgeon's personal life was in the realm of guidance. At various crisis points in his ministry it was so often biblical testimony which determined his decisions. When he was the teenage pastor of the Baptist chapel at Waterbeach, much pressure was put on him by his family and others to undertake formal training for the ministry. One day, with this as a burden on his mind, he was walking across Midsummer Common in Cambridge. As he did so the words of Jeremiah 45:5, which he knew by heart, came suddenly to him, 'Seekest thou great things for thyself? Seek them not!' Many years later he was to say, 'Had it not been for those words, in all probability I had never been where and what I am now.'[3] The remembrance of that one verse was decisive.

A no less critical point occurred in October 1856, at the height of Spurgeon's popularity during his third year in London. As he was leading a Sunday evening service in the Surrey Music Hall Gardens, packed with many thousands, a false cry of fire was raised in one of the galleries. Part of the congregation stampeded down staircases and in the excitement and confusion which followed seven people

---

[1] *The Treasury of David,* vol. 7 (London, 1890), p. v.

[2] It was published by Passmore and Alabaster in 1893. In a Preface, Mrs Spurgeon said, 'Surely the secret of his great strength lay in this, that he was willing to say what God put in his heart, and did not seek to use "enticing words of man's wisdom".'

[3] *C. H. Spurgeon: The Early Years,* p. 208.

were killed and more injured. The preacher was at some distance from the gallery where this happened and, not suspecting the disaster that was taking place out of sight, he continued with the service. When news was at length brought to him he collapsed from the shock, and his condition proved so serious that it was feared he might never preach again. In his own words, the catastrophe 'might have been sufficient to shatter my reason'.

His engagements were cancelled and he went to stay in a friend's house at Croydon, utterly overcome and unable to attend to any duty. It was the manner of his deliverance which is relevant to our present subject. It came not through reading Scripture but by Scripture which was in his heart and which broke in upon his desolation as he was alone in this friend's garden. The words brought to his mind were these: 'Wherefore God also hath highly exalted him, and given him a name which is above every name; that at the name of Jesus every knee should bow, of things in heaven, and things on earth, and things under the earth; and that every tongue should confess that Jesus Christ is Lord, to the glory of God the Father.' Instantly the assurance came to him afresh that Christ would certainly triumph over all. In that same moment he forgot himself and the clouds that had hung over him were gone. Christ was at the right hand of the Father and that was all he needed to know. When he returned to his pulpit these words from Philippians chapter two were his text. 'In a great measure,' he told his people, it was these words which 'enabled me to come here today'.

The Down-Grade controversy, of which I have written elsewhere, was almost certainly the greatest trial of his life and again it was by trust in the words of Scripture that he came through. From it came his book of daily promises, *The Cheque Book of the Bank of Faith*, concerning which he said: 'During his bitterest season of trial, the writer has stayed himself upon the Lord, and trusted his sacred promises.'[1]

Christians have trials of many kinds but Spurgeon believed that peace of mind comes from faith in the Word of God in all circumstances and on all occasions. Spiritual stability and the right use of Scripture go together: 'Ye are strong and the word of God abideth in you' (*1 John* 2:14). 'A true love for the great Book will bring us great peace from the great God. Nothing is a stumbling-block to the man who has the Word of God dwelling in him richly.'[2] So he knew no better summary of Christian duty than the description of it given by a Southern slave who, when witnessing to his happiness, declared, 'Massa, I fall flat on de promise'. Spurgeon made so much of the promises of God in his public ministry, and in his writings, because this was the way he had learned to live himself. In the pulpit he was sparing in references to himself but when he did so it was generally to show how he depended on what he preached to others. At the age of fifty-one, for example, preaching on the words, 'I will never leave thee, nor forsake thee' (*Heb.* 13:5), he said:

'I will tell you this morsel of my own faults: sometimes I have said, "I suffer so much. I am become so ill. I shall be so long away from the Tabernacle. The congregation will be greatly injured. Perhaps I shall never be able to preach again." I have struggled to this pulpit when I could scarcely

---

[1] *ST*, 1888, p. 507.
[2] *The Cheque Book of the Bank of Faith*, p. 100.

stand, and when the service was over, and I have been weary, the wicked whisper has come, "Yes, I shall soon be useless. I shall have to keep to my bed, or be wheeled about in a chair, and be a burden instead of a help." This has seemed a dreadful prospect; but "I will never leave thee, nor forsake thee," has come in, and I have shaken off my fears, and have rejoiced in the Lord my God."[1]

In many similar sermons, while there are no allusions to himself, it is clear that his own experience lay behind all he said and he regarded that fact as axiomatic for all preachers: 'True preaching is Artesian: it wells up from the great depths of the soul ... We are not proper agents for conveying truth to others, if grace has not conveyed it to us.'[2]

### The Bible and Future Revival

As we have already noted above, the latter years of Spurgeon's life were the most difficult for him. Instead of regarding him as a leader in evangelical belief, many now thought of him as an obstinate spokesman for a bygone era, 'the last of the Puritans'. Within his lifetime multitudes of professing Christians had passed from Calvinism to Arminianism, and from Arminianism to doubting the full inspiration of the Bible. Not even convictions concerning the full deity of Christ and his substitutionary death were secure in the prevailing miasma of learned unbelief. 'At first, Calvinism was too harsh, then evangelical doctrines became too antiquated, and now the Scriptures themselves must bow to man's alteration and improvement.'[3] 'We used to debate upon particular and general redemption, but

---

[1] *MTP*, vol. 32, p. 47.    [2] *MTP*, vol. 35, p. 615.
[3] *Only a Prayer Meeting*, p. 13.

now men question whether there is any redemption at all worthy of the name.'[1]

The burden of this situation would have been less for Spurgeon had he not believed that the condition of the church affects not only her own generation but those that follow. Compromise today is bound to have consequences tomorrow. But, while unable to avoid the conviction that the immediate future would not be bright, he did not believe that the Bible authorised pessimism. The cause of Christ was not at its end. The Word of God would break forth again among the nations. The Holy Spirit remained able to flood the world with a baptism of power and knowledge. Men would be convinced afresh that Christ is not in the tomb but in the midst of the throne which governs the universe. Thus, although he could say, 'What is being done today will affect the next centuries, unless the Lord should very speedily come,' he did not stop there: 'For my part, I am quite willing to be eaten of dogs for the next fifty years; but the more distant future shall vindicate me.'[2] 'If I must be the last of the Puritans, I will not be ashamed of it. My Lord will revive his buried truth as sure as he is God; the present madness will cease with its own short hour.'[3] The

---

[1] *ST*, 1888, p. 259.

[2] *An All-Round Ministry*, p. 360. His reference to Christ's second coming is important but he never allowed prophetical opinions as to its time to govern his outlook. 'There are brethren who can map out unfulfilled prophecy with great distinctness; but I confess my inability to do so' (*MTP*, vol. 33, p. 62). I have dealt more largely with his views on prophecy in *The Puritan Hope: Revival and the Interpretation of Prophecy* (Banner of Truth, 1971), pp. 256–65.

[3] *MTP*, vol. 30, p. 680. 'They look upon us as a benighted, old-fashioned Puritan, almost beneath their scorn; and we are grateful to

sermons of his closing years abound with a hope born from the promises of Scripture:

'Because the good old cause does not seem to prosper for a single day, and the kingdom does not come to Christ in my short life, shall I sit down and weep? Nay, I am but one amongst millions who shall achieve the divine purpose – one little coral insect, helping to pile up the rock on which, by and by, shall grow the cedar and the palm tree, and the lovely flowers ... I will do my work, though it be beneath the waves; I will do my work and die; and others shall do the same, but the rock is rising, God's purpose is being accomplished. In the words of the prayer of Moses, "Let thy work appear unto thy servants, and thy glory unto their children".

'Lord, let us take the work, and give our children the glory. Let us work on; they shall live to see the glory. Some future generation shall see the triumph ... Glory be to God, the victory is secure. Let us work on till then.'[1]

Spurgeon knew that the church could have the letter of Scripture without the Holy Spirit and without the manifest presence of Christ. Knowledge of the text of the Bible is not enough. But he had no sympathy with the idea of any

---

them for this unconscious witness to our fidelity'(*ST*, 1888, p. 91). According to 'the gentlemen who glory in "modern thought",' Spurgeon wrote at the end of his life, 'there are no Calvinists now alive with the exception of some half-dozen fools' (*ST*, 1892, p. 7).

[1] *MTP*, vol. 60, p. 548. 'What if the growing error of the age should have silenced the last tongue that speaks out the old gospel, let not faith be weakened. I hear the tramp of legions of soldiers of the cross. Let us fall back on the eternal God and never be discouraged for an instant' (*MTP*, vol. 32, p. 488). For other examples of the same, see *MTP*, vol. 33, p. 149; vol. 34, p. 550; vol. 38, pp. 257–8.

work of divine grace which did not proceed upon the basis of a believing acceptance of the Word of God. It was because the church of the Victorian era had allowed itself to be impressed by that which did not have the warrant of Scripture that she wandered as she did. To trust in Christ without believing obedience to his word is to trust in a delusion. Spurgeon taught his people to plead for revival and, just because he believed in revival, he did all in his power to see that a biblical witness would survive for the day when 'a new generation will arise strong in the Scriptures to purify the church and rid it of its false teachers.'

This book is not about Calvinism and Arminianism. Our concern in the following pages is to deal with the error that lies on the side of Calvinism furthest from Arminianism. But one point needs to be made here on the manner in which Arminianism affects the understanding of revival. Special times of blessing which we call revival are times which see an enlargement of the Spirit's *normal* work. That being so it must follow that, when the church's understanding of the Spirit's normal work is wrong, her understanding of revival will also be wrong. Is it the normal work of the Spirit to convert sinners *whenever they* decide upon it? Can men be born again by their own resolution? If the answer is 'Yes', and if that is how we are to understand Scripture, then it follows that we will look upon revivals simply as times when many make that choice. It was because such a deduction was based upon a wrong understanding of conversion in the last century that people began to see no difference between evangelistic campaigns and revivals; they became regarded as synonymous and capable of being organised by the same means. But if we believe the work of conversion is a work beyond all human ability, and that it requires an act of creative power giving life to the dead, then times of revival will be seen as times which can no more be 'promoted' than can the conversion of a single individual. Certainly the church must labour at all times for the salvation of the lost but whether in the case of one or of hundreds, 'the increase' belongs finally with God (*1 Cor.* 3:6).

Spurgeon believed that it was a departure from the doctrines of grace which had both prepared the way for the doctrinal slide and was leading evangelicals to confuse 'revivalism' with 'a work of a supernatural kind, putting power into the preaching of the Word, inspiring all believers with heavenly energy, and solemnly affecting the careless, so that they may turn to God and live.'[1] He believed that it would be the recovery of a more scriptural doctrine of conversion, putting God at the head of things, which would be found in great revivals of the future. When they would come he did not pretend to know but it would be through the risen Christ owning his own word. From the text, 'And he had in his hand seven stars: and out of his mouth went a sharp two-edged sword' (*Rev.* 1:16), he gave his people this certainty:

'The church will never make any great advance until

---

[1] *Only a Prayer-Meeting,* pp. 12–13. 'I am very fearful that many so-called "revivals" have, in the long run, wrought more harm than good.' He was referring to the kind of methods which had replaced a biblical understanding of conversion with decisionism. 'If we are to obtain a revival we must go directly to the Holy Ghost for it, and not resort to the machinery of the professional revival-maker' (*ST*, 1866, p. 532). I discuss this further in *Revival and Revivalism: the Making and Marring of American Evangelicalism* (Banner of Truth, 1994).

once more God sends here and there, and in fifty places, men with burning hearts and trumpet voices to proclaim the truth, the whole truth, and nothing but the truth. We need men that will not yield to the current of the times, nor care one iota about it: but will hold their own and hold their Master's Word against all comers, because the Lord of hosts is with them, and the Spirit of Christ resteth upon them. I would have you at this time realize the Christ with the seven stars in his hand, and I would have you pray, "Lord, fill thy hand with the stars again. Light up the darkness of this period with flaming preachers of thy word to the praise of the glory of thy grace".[1]

[1] *MTP*, vol. 33, p. 39.

## 2

## *An Impression of Spurgeon in Early Years by F. Curtis*[1]

Before closing my reminiscences of my unmarried life, I wish to record my experience of Spurgeon as a preacher, which for several reasons was very interesting to myself.

I first heard him preach in 1857, when with my mother and younger sister I was staying with kind friends in Ladbroke Square, Notting Hill. Spurgeon was at that time holding his services in the vast Vauxhall glass-palace, where he habitually addressed ten thousand people.[2] He was then, I should think, about two-and-twenty, and already at the zenith of his fame. Though decidedly plain, at that age his face was to me attractive, the square forehead and magnificent dark eyes redeeming it from ugliness, and every line of his face and figure speaking of power. In that enormous building, his solitary voice led the singing. With arms outstretched, beating time with his hymn book, he

---

[1] This graphic description by a contemporary does not appear to have been used previously in books on Spurgeon. It was published by the author, Mrs F. Curtis, in her privately printed *Memories of a Long Life,* 1912, pp. 141–7.

[2] The reference is to the Music Hall, Surrey Gardens, which contained upwards of 6,000 feet of glass. Spurgeon preached there for three years from 19 October 1856.

kept the huge mass of voices together, his own voice pre-dominating without an effort. I remember a distinguished foreigner writing in the newspapers that the singing of hymns by Spurgeon's congregation was the finest thing he had heard in England.

There were three galleries in the building, which were all crammed. In a front seat in the gallery opposite to us were the chief members of the Cabinet, who came Sunday after Sunday, perhaps more to take lessons in eloquence than for their souls' profit. We went early, but it was impossible to obtain a seat, and I stood for two hours without the slightest fatigue, being so supported by the crowd that pressed around me that no weight rested on my feet. I forget the subject of the sermon, but remember the preacher by no means objected to the bursts of laughter following the witticisms by which he enlivened his discourse, solemn and even tremendous as its chief topics were. But the chief impression left upon my mind was the absolute hold of the speaker upon his audience. Not an eye wandered, not for a moment was attention relaxed. Such popularity as Spurgeon now enjoyed was an ordeal which any man's character for simplicity and integrity could hardly be expected to survive, and one could scarcely wonder that a stern and pessimistic bishop with Evan-gelical views should say to his chaplain, 'You watch that man, you will see he will have a great fall.' But Spurgeon did not fall. He was doubtless upheld mainly by the energy of godliness which was the ruling principle of his life, but he was also supported by a bulwark of common sense. He married the right woman as early as possible in his career, and though a devoted husband, he was emphatically not a 'woman's man' but a 'man's man', carefully avoiding the enervating influence of feminine blandishment. He was honest to the core, attacking forcibly, when necessary, those whose favour was most important to him. Furthermore, he had no artificial standard of godliness. He did not measure sanctity by rules of dress or speech, but went straight for the realities of Christian living – truth, honesty, love for God and man. He was no ascetic, nor did he aim at singularity. I remember a critical observer making the remark, 'Spurgeon is no better than other people; I see him every day on the top of a bus, smoking among all the other men.' The 'other men' were doubtless aware of the reality in him which had escaped the religious critic.

His printed sermons have had an influence not limited by the horizon of his own persuasion. They have leavened the teaching of many who are furthest from his ecclesiastical position. In a remote district of Cumberland I met a very High Church parson who told me he never wrote a sermon without first reading one of Spurgeon's. As an instance of the hold they have had on a lower class, I mention the following experience of my friend Mr Aldous, of Sheffield. When in London on one occasion, he was passing through a very low by-street connecting two principal thoroughfares. He turned into a little grocer's shop to buy some trifle, and on the counter he saw a large pile of Spurgeon's last Sunday's sermon. He bought one, and was so impressed by it that he returned to the shop next day for another copy, but all were sold. What an amount of good leaven must thus have been spread among a class which might never have been reached in any other way.

I did not hear Spurgeon again for many years. It was, I think, in 1865, that he gave an address and held a service in

Sheffield Town Hall, and in company with Mr Aldous I went to hear him. All the attraction of his youthful appearance had vanished. He was coarse-looking even to grossness, heavy in form and features, yet as soon as he spoke, one felt the same power was there and that the man himself was unchanged. Sheffield Town Hall, being a secular building, was on this occasion treated with scant respect as a place of worship. The gallery behind the speaker's platform was crowded by specimens of Sheffield's roughest class. They kept their hats on, and talked and laughed audibly until the preacher appeared. Looking up at the gallery filled with this irreverent mob, he said, 'Before I proceed further I wish to remark that it is customary when any religious service is held for Christian men to remove their hats. Any Jewish friends who are present will, of course, keep their hats on.' In an instant every hat was removed, a low titter betraying that the humour of the situation was appreciated. Mr Aldous' remark was, 'I should not have thought it was within the power of any mortal man to make a Sheffield mob take off their hats.' The behaviour in the gallery was thenceforward most decorous, the men recognising that they had met their master.

In the course of his address he related the following incident. 'I was having a talk with a man who was young, rich, and in the enjoyment of every good thing this world could give him, and who maintained that religion was a melancholy thing. "I cannot stand your Christian people," he said, "their religion does not make them cheerful or agreeable, and they are always in trouble, moaning and groaning and complaining." "Come along with me, my friend," I said, "we will visit one of your complaining

Christians." I took him to a wretched fireless garret, where beside the empty grate sat a poor old woman, doubled up with rheumatism, and groaning with the pain. "Oh," she said, "it is so bad, and it never gets any better." "Well, my friend," I said, "look at this young man. He is rich, he is healthy and strong, he has every pleasure that earth can give him, and he is without God in the world. Tell me now, would you change with him?" *"Change with him!"*'

A great sob burst from the audience. The stalwart man beside me was in tears. They were but three words, but spoken with thrilling emphasis they pierced to the very joints and marrow, and they will never be forgotten.

I never afterwards came across Spurgeon, though I have derived much help from his printed sermons.

# PART TWO

## *The Controversy with Hyper-Calvinism*

'I do not think I differ from any of my Hyper-Calvinistic brethren in what I do believe, but I differ from them in what they do not believe. I do not hold any less than they do, but I hold a little more, and, I think, a little more of the truth revealed in the Scriptures. Not only are there a few cardinal points of doctrine by which we can steer our ship North, South, East, or West, but as we study the Word, we shall begin to learn something about North-west and North-east, and all else that lies between the four cardinal points.'

C. H. Spurgeon
*The Early Years,* p. 173.

'Hyper-Calvinism is all house and no door; Arminianism is all door and no house.'

John Duncan, *Life of John Duncan*
David Brown (Edinburgh, 1872), p. 404.

# 3

# *The Combatants and the Cause of the Controversy*

When we think of the millions of words that have been written and spoken about Spurgeon since his lifetime, it is noteworthy that very little attention appears to have been given to what his *Autobiography* called 'the first serious attack' on his preaching.[1] W. Y. Fullerton, one of his best-known biographers, passed over it in a couple of paragraphs and thought the whole matter 'makes quaint reading'.[2] Lewis Drummond's recent work on Spurgeon extends to more than eight hundred pages, yet he also scarcely touches on this first controversy and supposes that it merely involved 'differences in finer theological points'.[3] Contrary to such opinions, it can be argued that behind this 'first serious attack' lay issues of major importance. Too often it has been supposed that the difference between Calvinism and Hyper-Calvinism is

[1] *C. H. Spurgeon's Autobiography*, vol. 2, p. 35. Most, if not all, of my quotations from this source can also be found in the two-volume revised edition, *The Early Years* and *The Full Harvest* (Banner of Truth, 1962 and 1973) currently in print.

[2] W. Y. Fullerton, *C. H. Spurgeon, A Biography* (London: Williams and Norgate, 1920), p. 290.

[3] Lewis A. Drummond, *Spurgeon, Prince of Preachers* (Grand Rapids: Kregel, 1992), p. 558.

simply a question of degree. Perhaps the very labels themselves are unfortunate, for the prefix to the latter – 'hyper', from the Greek, 'above' or 'beyond' – may suggest simply a difference only in degree, somewhat like the difference in height between the ceilings of two chapels. That is not the case as Spurgeon made clear by insisting that the real difference was between 'true' Calvinism and 'false'.[1] At the same time he was also careful to say that his use of the word Calvinism did not mean that he used the name of the sixteenth-century reformer as though it was the standard for truth. The label was simply intended to designate 'that glorious system which teaches that salvation is of grace from first to last',[2] and 'while Calvin is nobody to us', he was sure that the reformer's teaching was not that of the Hyper-Calvinists.

The fact that Spurgeon's controversy with Hyper-Calvinism has been treated with such lack of interest since his death is not without significance. For most of the years that have passed since then true Calvinism has been in eclipse and, as Hyper-Calvinism is an aberration from true Calvinism, it is not surprising that it has also fallen into obscurity. Hyper-Calvinism only arises whenever and wherever the truth of the sovereignty of God in salvation is firmly believed. The reason why Spurgeon's first controversy has been so little thought of in these last hundred years is not that the subject is insignificant. It is rather that doctrinal Christianity as a whole has been too largely ignored. At the present time, when evangelical Calvinism is again being recovered in many parts of the earth, the

[1] *NPSP*, vol. 4 (London, 1859: Banner of Truth, 1964), p. 341.
[2] *MTP*, vol. 7, p. 302.

danger of Hyper-Calvinism is once more a possibility and the lessons to be drawn from this old controversy have again become relevant.

Before we come to the controversy itself there are one or two preliminary things to be considered by way of background. The first concerns the three men who were key figures in the debate. They were James Wells, Charles Waters Banks and Spurgeon himself. All three were pastors of London Baptist churches and we must start with brief portraits of each of them in turn.

At the date of this first attack, referred to above, Spurgeon was twenty years of age. Only nine months before he had been settled as the pastor of the historic congregation which met close to the south bank of the Thames in New Park Street, Southwark. It was in this same month of January 1855 that his sermons began to be printed every week and the youth, who only a year before had been an unknown stranger in London, was already becoming something of a celebrity. His congregation was one of about 1,370 Baptist congregations in England, all of which were Calvinistic or 'Particular' (i.e., holding to particular over against universal redemption).[1] These churches could hardly be called a denomination in the normal sense of that term for there was no overall structure and too much independence existed to make the 'union' which had been organised in 1813, and again in 1831, very popular

[1] The Religious Census of 1851 noted 1,374 Particular Baptist chapels in England. The New Connexion Baptists (Arminian) had 179 chapels, and the Old General Baptists (largely Unitarian) 93. Many Particular Baptist churches were also 'Strict', that is to say, only professing Christians baptised by immersion were admitted to membership and the Lord's table. See below p. 158.

or effective. Certainly New Park Street Chapel had required no approval from anyone to install their teenage pastor.

It was common knowledge that Spurgeon had not grown up as a Particular Baptist, and G. H. Pike says that at the outset of his London ministry no one was sure where his future affiliations would lie in terms of other congregations.[1] 'I care not for any denomination or party,' Spurgeon could tell his congregation in 1858.[2]

James Wells (1803–1872) may be little known today but in 1855 Spurgeon had reason to refer to him in private as 'King James'.[3] As with many famous men, Wells had more than one nickname. One newspaper said that he was commonly known as 'Wheelbarrow Wells' but it did not tell us why. In his youth he had been a carrier delivering parcels in London and perhaps a wheelbarrow had preceded the days when he drove a horse and cart. It is easier to understand why Banks called him 'the Borough Gunner'. Wells' church, also on the south side of the Thames, was the Surrey Tabernacle in Borough High Street, and something akin to gunfire was not infrequently heard from its pulpit. Its pastor was a self-made, self-educated man, of outstanding natural talents and enormous energy. He was fifty-one when the controversy now before us began and had been the most popular Baptist preacher south of the river since his arrival there more than thirty years earlier. Twice his church building had

[1] G. H. Pike, *Life and Work of C. H. Spurgeon,* vol. 1 (London: Cassell, 1894; repr. Banner of Truth, 1991), p. 148. Hereafter cited as 'Pike'.

[2] *NPSP*, vol. 4, p. 344.

[3] Letter of 1 January 1855 to his wife (*Autobiography*, vol. 2, p. 19).

been enlarged and still it remained full with about 1,200 people. Pike referred to him as 'a pulpit genius of great powers' and 'the ablest man of his denomination'.[1] Banks, speaking of Wells in 1855, wrote, 'We know his talent is great; his influence is immense; his success as a minister is, in these days, almost without parallel, and our love to, and esteem for him, is *sincere, permanent, and practical.*'[2] In a different vein, a writer in the *Gospel Standard* was to recall the Surrey Tabernacle preacher in these words: 'No man ever lashed the Arminians more severely or more effectually than he did. "I have been used to carrying a whip," he would say, "and I must whip these free-willers"'.[3] Wells died in 1872 and it was typical that the last Sunday morning he was in his pulpit, his sermon lasted for one hour twenty minutes!

Charles Waters Banks (1806–1886) was a friend of Wells but the two men differed in some respects, not least in their size. Banks was a diminutive five-foot three. The photograph of him which has survived shows a kindness in his face that is borne out in all that we know of him. Like Wells, he was also a popular London preacher, though his pulpit at Unicorn Yard Chapel did not major in artillery fire. In a tribute after his death he was remembered, among others things, for his 'breadth of kindness, meekness and forbearance towards others.' Banks' congregation, like that of New Park Street, was in Southwark, and it was characteristic of the man that he was one of the first of the older ministers to befriend Spurgeon. Pike calls

[1] Pike, vol. 1, p. 147; vol. 2, p. 281.
[2] *Earthen Vessel; and Christian Record and Review* (London), 1855, p. 14.
[3] *Gospel Standard*, October 1874, pp. 407–8.

Banks 'Mr Spurgeon's early London friend',[1] and it is said that at this date Spurgeon was 'a frequent visitor' at Banks' home in Bermondsey New Road.[2] The year of Spurgeon's settlement at New Park Street, 1854, was also 'the cholera year' in London and labouring in the midst of a common suffering brought the two men closer together. Banks himself had cholera. When Spurgeon fell ill, Banks called on him and the time of prayer they then had together was never to be forgotten. 'The communion and prayer at the bedside was so sacred and sweet,' that when Banks rose from his knees, 'Mr Spurgeon exclaimed, with the tears running down his youthful-looking face, "What a Patmos!"'[3]

Banks was a man with many irons in the fire. Preaching was his first love. He itinerated far and wide, reportedly travelling an annual average of 12,000 miles for thirty years. But the printing press was a close second. Before his conversion he had been a printer and journalist and from 1843, the year he began preaching in London, he seems to have turned his home into both a print shop and a publisher's office. John Banks, his son, speaks of their being up all night to produce the first issue of the *Earthen Vessel* in time for publication to commence on 1 December, 1843. For forty-three years Banks was to

[1] Pike, vol. 1, p. 146.

[2] *Earthen Vessel,* 1892, 'The Late Mr C. H. Spurgeon, Personal Recollections', J. W. Banks, pp. 93–4.

[3] *Ibid.*, p. 93. Perhaps Spurgeon's 'illness' was more exhaustion and temporary depression. 'My friends seemed falling one by one, and I felt or fancied that I was sickening like those around me. A little more work and weeping would have laid me low among the rest' (*Autobiography,* vol. 1, p. 371).

continue producing and editing this monthly magazine. On the night of his death in 1886 he had been sitting up in bed only a few hours before, 'surrounded with letters, pen, ink, and all the concomitants of an editor's room.' It is astonishing that the production of one magazine was not enough for Banks. For thirty-six years he was also the editor of *Cheering Words* and when Spurgeon first knew him he also produced what his son believed to be 'the first penny weekly religious paper ever printed', entitled the *Christian Cabinet.* A common concern to publish Calvinistic and evangelical material brought Banks and Spurgeon closer together and it was probably in the pages of the *Christian Cabinet* that Spurgeon first wrote for the press. John Banks, who was in his twenties at the time when his father's friendship with the young preacher began, says of Spurgeon: 'I well remember his lively and cheerful manner, and the pleasantry of his conversation to us as he stood by the printing press while we were printing our favourite magazine.'

But if the printing press at first drew the two men closer it was also to be the occasion of the controversy which we are to consider. The 7,000 monthly purchasers of the *Earthen Vessel* were largely made up of Particular and Strict Baptists, and Banks knew that there was an unease among a number of them over the new pastor of New Park Street. To help remove doubts, and to express his own esteem for his friend, Banks wrote a six-and-half page article in the December 1854 issue of the *Earthen Vessel* entitled, 'A Brief and Impartial View of Mr Spurgeon's Ministry'. He also had another purpose in view. As he told his readers: 'We are disposed to believe there is truth in the statement of a correspondent – he says – *"I believe Mr*

*Spurgeon is as great a lover of free grace and of real Calvinism, as any man;* but the bigotry of some, who cannot hear the truth unless expressed in certain phrases, seems to put him out of heart; and keeps him walking almost in a separate path."[1] Banks, like the correspondent he quoted, clearly wanted Spurgeon to be brought more to the centre of Particular Baptist witness. His 'Impartial View' included some words of caution with respect to aspects of Spurgeon's ministry and he did not deny that there was evidence of immaturity. Yet his words were largely supportive of 'the young man' whose 'labours have been amazingly successful in raising up the before drooping cause at Park Street.' His assessment concluded: 'Should his life be spared, and his soul's experience of divine things be deepened, we believe that when many of us are silent in the grave, he will be found of great use in the church of Jesus Christ.'[2]

To this commendation of Spurgeon, 'King James' of the Surrey Tabernacle at once replied in tones of thunder in the January 1855 issue of the *Earthen Vessel*. Far from agreeing with Banks, Wells believed that the newcomer's preaching was dangerous, superficial and deceptive. Spurgeon's natural gifts were indeed indisputable but Wells had doubts whether he was converted and warned, 'A man cannot preach with any success what he does not know.'[3] A major controversy had begun.

\* \* \*

[1] *Earthen Vessel*, 1854, p. 279.  [2] *Earthen Vessel*, 1854, p. 283.
[3] *Earthen Vessel*, 1855, p. 16.

Before we look at this controversy in more detail it is important to give some consideration to why it happened. The simplest explanation is that it was a personality clash between an older and a younger preacher, with Banks caught in the middle. Banks himself in his 'Impartial View' had brought the two preachers' names together in a sentence in which he said, 'We know of no Baptist minister in all the metropolis – (with the exception of our highly favoured and long-tried brother James Wells, of Surrey Tabernacle,) – who has such crowded auditories and continued overflowing congregations, as Mr Spurgeon has.'[1] The secular press did not doubt that mere ambition was the cause of the clash. The *Lambeth Gazette* reported:

'The Rev. C. H. Spurgeon is now the star of Southwark. Mr Wells of the Borough Road, has, for some years past, had the run in this line; but he has, at last, got a rival well up in his "tip", and likely to prove the favourite for a long time.'[2]

Apocryphal stories on the supposed antagonism between the two men began to spread. Simple though this explanation is, it is not the truth. No doubt, as with every Christian, Wells was a man of imperfect sanctification, and he displayed an imperfect spirit in controversy, but the evidence points to his being a man of upright and sincere principles. Banks specifically rejects the accusation that the pastor of Surrey Tabernacle was antagonised by Spurgeon's rising fame. There is no indication that Spurgeon believed that charge. Although 'the two men had not very

[1] *Earthen Vessel*, 1854, p. 277.

[2] *Lambeth Gazette*, 1 September 1855, quoted in *Autobiography*, vol. 2, pp. 56–7.

much in common',[1] John Banks believed, 'Mr Spurgeon always held the late James Wells in high esteem, as I remember him saying in New Park-street pulpit, "I love Mr Wells as a brother in Christ," and this attitude was maintained till Mr Wells' death.'[2]

The fundamental explanation of the controversy is that Wells sincerely believed that the Calvinistic witness which he had sought to maintain in London for over a quarter of a century was the only genuine Calvinism. He cannot have been ignorant that a number had questioned whether that witness, which had come down, with variations, through such men as John Gill and William Huntington,[3] was not, in part, an aberration from orthodoxy, but that was a question for which he had no sympathy at all. He was assured that to depart from it would be to depart from Scripture. For him the idea that all men should be called to faith in Christ, as Spurgeon preached, was 'Fullerism', that is to say, the 'error' introduced among the Baptists by Andrew Fuller (1754–1815) and his 'mongrel Calvinist' friends towards the end of the previous century. Christ is only the Saviour of the elect and therefore it cannot be the duty of the non-elect to believe in him for a salvation not provided for them. To assert the opposite was stigmatised as 'duty-faith' error. Wells' people, it was said, regarded him as sent of God to 'knock down a "duty-faith" system and wheel away the rubbish.'[4]

---

[1] Williams, *Personal Reminiscences,* p. 61. The same author noted two meetings between the two preachers.

[2] *Earthen Vessel,* 1892, p. 92.

[3] For Gill and Huntington, see below, pp. 125–39.

[4] Pike, vol. 2, p. 281, quoting a writer in the *Earthen Vessel.*

From the outset of his ministry in south London Spurgeon knew that there was a type of Calvinism popular in Baptist chapels different from his own. He wrote to his father in December 1853: 'The London people are rather higher in Calvinism than I am: but I have succeeded in bringing one church to my own views, and will trust, with Divine assistance, to do the same with another. I am a Calvinist; I love what someone called "glorious Calvinism", but "Hyperism" is too hot for my palate.'[1]

It is an extraordinary misrepresentation of the case that the well-known Baptist history by A. C. Underwood can attribute the cause of Spurgeon's first controversy to his departure from *Calvinism*. This modern Baptist historian writes:

'The truth seems to be that the old Calvinistic phrases were often on Spurgeon's lips but the genuine Calvinistic meaning had gone out of them. This explains the attacks made upon him, as soon as he began his ministry in London, by those who had never departed from an un-adulterated Calvinism.'[2]

These words are typical of those who cannot see any difference between Calvinism and Hyper-Calvinism. The real explanation of the controversy was that, even at the age of twenty, Spurgeon knew enough about the history of evangelicalism to believe that it was the south-bank theology of Wells and others which was the real innovation. His knowledge came in part from his own denominational

---

[1] *Autobiography*, vol. 1, p. 342.

[2] A. C. Underwood, *A History of the English Baptists* (London: Baptist Union Publications Dept., 1947), p. 204. On all matters affecting biblical doctrine Underwood is unreliable.

background among Congregational chapels which had
been unaffected by the rise of Hyper-Calvinism among the
Calvinistic Baptists of the eighteenth century. Soon after he
had joined the Baptists, Spurgeon had come across Hyper-
Calvinism and evidence that its influence was inimical to
evangelism. One hearer at least in his Waterbeach pastorate
had called him 'a Fullerite'.[1] Spurgeon was conscious of
this critical element when he preached one of his early sermons in his first pastorate on, 'All that the Father giveth me
shall come to me; and him that cometh to me I will in no
wise cast out' (*John* 6:37). He introduced his text with the
words, 'Surely this passage will suit all, from the "Hyper"
down to the Primitive [Methodist].' At the end of his notes
on this same sermon he wrote this private comment:

'Read, write, print, shout, – *"Him that cometh to Me I
will in no wise cast out."* Great Saviour, I thank Thee for
this text; help Thou me so to preach from it that many may
come to Thee, and find eternal life!'[2]

From his own early reading of the Puritans, Spurgeon
was convinced that they were no supporters of the beliefs
which Hyper-Calvinists claimed – 'I have all the Puritans
with me – the whole of them without a single exception.'[3]
He believed that Fuller had been correct in his assertion
made in 1787 that 'no writer of eminence can be named
before the present century, who denied it to be the duty of
men in general to believe in the Lord Jesus Christ for the
salvation of their souls.'[4] So-called 'Fullerism' represented

---

[1] *Autobiography*, vol. 1, p. 256.
[2] *Autobiography*, vol. 1, pp. 225–6.     [3] *MTP*, vol. 7, p. 148.
[4] From Fuller's *Defence of a Treatise Entitled the Gospel Worthy of
All Acceptation*, quoted by J. W. Morris, *Memoirs of Andrew Fuller*
(London, 1816), p. 263. Spurgeon refers to Fuller as 'that man of

an emphasis not only to be found in the Reformers and Puritans but supremely in Scripture itself.

For all his comparatively light-hearted words to his father in the letter quoted above, Spurgeon, equally with Wells, believed that serious principles were involved. It may be argued that the controversy that began in 1855 was bound to happen. Sooner or later someone had to challenge whether Hyper-Calvinism was the 'unadulterated' article. The last intention of Banks when he wrote his 'Impartial View' had been to start a storm, but once Wells read it and its opinion that Spurgeon was emphasising 'what ministers of truth, in our time, have long neglected to enforce',[1] a disturbance was inevitable.

---

God' (*MTP*, vol. 13, p. 719) whereas William Gadsby called him 'the greatest enemy the church of God ever had, as his sentiments were so much cloaked with the sheep's clothing' (W. Gadsby, *Works*, vol. 1 [London, 1851], p. 27. Quoted by R. W. Oliver in 'The Significance of Strict Baptist Attitudes towards Duty Faith in the Nineteenth Century', *Strict Baptist Historical Society Bulletin,* No. 20, 1993).

For proof that the claim of Spurgeon and Fuller was correct one has only to turn to the Articles of the Synod of Dort (1619) which include the words: 'As many as are called by the gospel are unfeignedly called; for God hath most earnestly and truly declared in his Word what will be acceptable to him, namely, that all who are called should comply with the invitation. He, moreover, seriously promises eternal life and rest to as many as shall come to him and believe on him. It is not the fault of the gospel, nor of Christ offered therein, nor of God, who calls men by the gospel, and confers upon them various gifts, that those who are called by the ministry of the Word refuse to come and be converted. The fault lies in themselves.' (Philip Schaff, *A History of the Creeds of Christendom,* [London, 1878], vol. 1, p. 522).

[1] *Earthen Vessel*, 1854, p. 277.

# 4

## *The Case Against Spurgeon*

Information on the controversy which began in 1855 has come down to us chiefly in Banks' magazine, the *Earthen Vessel* and in Spurgeon's published sermons. For the case against Spurgeon we must go to the *Earthen Vessel* and for his own case we must go to the *New Park Street Pulpit* and to other parts of his published works.[1] In this chapter we will look at the controversy as it unfolded in the *Earthen Vessel*.

James Wells' response to Banks' 'Impartial View' of Spurgeon was written under the pseudonym of 'Job'. The pastor of Surrey Tabernacle had long contributed to the *Earthen Vessel* without using his own name. In the course of years he wrote no fewer than seventy letters on doctrinal subjects under the name of 'Theophilus' and for other material he supplied to Banks he had different pseudonyms. Probably the whole of south London, with Spurgeon, recognised that Job's response was written by Wells. Banks must have been taken aback by its strength. Wells had long been a friend and colleague and not to print him would have been unthinkable. Banks respected his

---

[1] Wells' sermons were also obviously involved but their weekly publication did not begin until 1859.

judgment and, in any case, it was always his policy to print more than one side on any question. Wells took the Spurgeon issue so seriously, that he regarded Banks' commendation as nothing less than a disastrous change of direction in the journal he had so long encouraged his whole party to support. In his published response of January 1855 he warned Banks that he had better understand that for many the future of the magazine had been brought into question:

'If the EARTHEN VESSEL intends to change Masters, let it do so at once, and the living in Jerusalem will have done with it ... If it grow lukewarm, and is neither hot nor cold, we must cast it out of our mouths, nor must we take up its name into our lips.'[1]

Banks did not let this reproof stand without editorial comment. He had introduced his assessment of Spurgeon into the magazine, he wrote, in response to 'many inquiries which arose in different quarters'. He had not sought the patronage of Mr Spurgeon and he was not going to be frightened by 'brother Job's' threat of 'discarding the VESSEL'. After hearing 'a great deal *for*' Spurgeon, 'and very much *against* him', he told his readers, he had prayerfully gone to listen for himself and had been blessed in doing so. 'We have therefore hoped, that God, even our God, had set him on the Walls of Zion, for usefulness and for real good to thousands of poor sinners. If we have erred the good Lord pardon us.'[2]

Later in 1855 Banks followed this up with three articles reviewing Spurgeon's *New Park Street Pulpit*, under the heading, 'The Gospel Ministry Carefully Considered'. In

[1] *Earthen Vessel,* 1855, p. 13.   [2] *Earthen Vessel,* 1855, p. 17.

these articles he first sought to show what are 'the evidences of a heaven-born and God-sent ministry'. The supreme evidence, he argued, was that it is life-giving, and this is what he found in the ministry of the New Park Street preacher. Many of his correspondents, Banks admitted, held an adverse opinion. In their view, Spurgeon's was 'a second-hand ministry, deeply tainted with an Arminian spirit'.[1] Banks challenged the truth of that opinion. His own conviction was now more definite:

'It was a nice opinion of Richard Sibbes when he said, "The office of a minister is to be a wooer, to make up the marriage between Christ and Christian souls:" and we will plainly speak our mind; – we have hoped, that C. H. Spurgeon's work, in the hands of the Holy Ghost, is to woo, and to win souls over to Jesus Christ; and we have an impression – should his life be spared, that, through his instrumentality – all our churches will, by and by, be increased. God Almighty grant that we may be true prophets; and then, to all our cruel correspondents we will say – fire away – cut up, cast out, and condemn THE EARTHEN VESSEL, much as ye may, ye will do us no harm. The temple of the Lord is being built ...

'In the course of Mr Spurgeon's ministry there are frequently to be found such gushings forth of love to God – of ravishing delights in Christ – of the powerful anointings of the Holy Ghost – as compel us to believe that God is in him of a truth. We must confess this is the deep-wrought conviction of our spirit; and we dare not conceal it. Why should we? We may be condemned by many; but, what-ever it may cost us – whoever may discard us – we must

[1] *Earthen Vessel,* 1855, p. 241.

acknowledge that, while in these sermons we have met with sentences that perplex us – and with what some might consider contradictions – still, we have found those things which have been powerful demonstrations of the indwelling of THE LIFE and THE LOVE of the triune God in the preacher's heart.'[1]

Banks was in a real difficulty; all his spiritual instincts told him that God was blessing the work at New Park Street and he loved the preacher who was being thus used. But there was no denying that the 'contradictions' to which he referred had long been regarded among many of the Particular Baptists as symptoms of defection from Calvinism. By his personal links with Spurgeon, Banks had also given the opportunity for some to suggest that he might be looking for the larger benefits which an identification with the famous young preacher could bring. In printing and publishing, as in other things, the two men might have become permanent collaborators. Referring to this point in later years, Banks' son wrote, 'If earthly objects had been my father's chief aim, a golden opportunity offered itself.'[2] But Banks was no self-seeker and he also believed that 'duty-faith' was an error. He did not intend to support Spurgeon on that issue. What he was trying to do in the controversy was to show that there was enough 'precious gospel' in what Spurgeon was preaching to warrant his being treated as a friend and ally.

For Wells the 'contradictions' in Spurgeon were too serious to tolerate such an attitude. He had correctly judged that Spurgeon was more likely to take numbers

---

[1] *Earthen Vessel*, 1855, pp. 202–3.
[2] *Earthen Vessel*, 1892, p. 93.

from his party rather than to be won to it himself (as Banks initially seemed to have hoped). After the initial confrontation in January 1855 Wells continued to write for Banks, usually under a pseudonym. Without mentioning Spurgeon by name he constantly came back to what he regarded as the main issue. He deplored the fact that 'great numbers of professing Christians ... hold that it is the duty of man savingly to believe in Christ, and that men are condemned for not having saving faith in Christ.'[1] 'The doctrine of duty-faith,' he says in another article, 'I throw to Paul's dung heap.'[2] For the moment the point was not taken up but in the January issue of 1857 it was, and that by a young man of the name of T. W. Medhurst, who had formerly attended Wells' church. While hearing Wells he had continued to live a worldly life; Sundays he gave to the Surrey Tabernacle and weekdays to the theatre. Describing how all this changed, Pike writes:

'Mr Medhurst was tempted to hear him [Spurgeon] at New Park Street Chapel. At first, however, he actually trembled at the thought of leaving a teacher so sound in the faith as James Wells to hear a mere Arminian like Spurgeon. It was leaving the assembly of the saints to hear an adventurer, who was giving the people a stone in place of bread ... The sermon happened to be one of a rousing kind, founded on Hosea 6:3 – "Then shall we know, if we follow on to know the Lord." It turned out that Mr Spurgeon was no Arminian after all; and the discourse made so deep an impression that the young tradesman gave

---

[1] *Earthen Vessel,* 1855, p. 283. Wells here writes, I believe, under the pseudonym, 'A Little One'.

[2] *Earthen Vessel,* 1856, p. 57.

up the theatre, and saw himself "a sinner, lost, ruined, undone."[1]

Medhurst said nothing of this in writing to the *Earthen Vessel* but instead he asked innocently:

'Why this blast and noise about duty-faith? Why do we not leave off bickering and quarrelling, and leave preachers to their God and their consciences, striving to rectify our own faults, and leave other people alone until we ourselves are perfect? Duty-faith, what is it? "Oh," says one, "it is an ugly hobgoblin, which is frightening half the parsons of the present day." Well, let us examine it. List; it speaks, "Believe and be saved; believe not, and be damned" – hoarse though the voice is, yet how marvellously it is like the *old book* – Mark 16:16. Well, duty-faith, we will let you alone, for if you be of God, you must stand; while, on the other hand, if you be of man you must fall.'

In the second half of his letter Medhurst went on to describe saving faith as 'a principle from God ... a mighty power, for when I enter into a corpse I bring with me life' – but the ears of many were already shut to his words. Banks, again, seems to have been taken by surprise at the degree of alarm which Medhurst had occasioned. True to his policy of allowing open discussion, he published a rebuttal of Medhurst in his February 1857 issue, prefacing it with

---

[1] Pike, vol. 2, p. 229. A fuller account of Medhurst's conversion can be found in an article by Pike in *ST*, 1877, pp. 9–15. The sermon by Spurgeon which brought him assurance was on 'him that cometh to me I will in no wise cast out' ( *John* 6:37). 'Hitherto he had committed the mistake [the influence of Wells' teaching] of trying to answer the question, "Am I one of the elect?" He now perceived that they are the elect who trust wholly in Christ.' For Medhurst see also *Letters of Charles Haddon Spurgeon* (Banner of Truth, 1992).

these words: 'We never expected for one moment, that the insertion of Mr Medhurst's letter, last month, would have been interpreted as, by some, it has been ... In our efforts we aim at the establishment of peace in our churches. But alas! we almost despair.'

A correspondent who answered Medhurst objected strongly to the hesitating tone in which the latter had written, as though it were an open question whether faith might be a duty. Saving faith in Christ cannot be the duty of sinners, he retorted, because if we exhort the dead in trespasses and sins to trust in Christ we are attributing a power to them which they do not have. The preaching of duty-faith, in his view, 'has done a world of mischief in our churches.' He argued that to speak 'to men personally and indiscriminately, exhorting them to believe and be saved etc.', is a misuse of Mark 16:16. That text, he argued, only shows what the preacher is to teach 'declaratively', that is to say, that believing in Christ is the *evidence* of salvation.[1]

Spurgeon's name was unmentioned but it reappeared in the May 1857 issue when Banks published correspondence between Joseph Wilkins, a Baptist pastor in Brighton, and James Wells. Wells had accepted an invitation to preach for Wilkins but then, on hearing that the latter was 'in close fellowship with Mr Spurgeon', he had withdrawn. Two letters by Wells to Wilkins were printed, and one by Wilkins, together with the enquiry of the correspondent who had provided the letters, 'whether Mr Wells be right or whether he be wrong?' The letters of Wells to Wilkins confirmed the main point of his objection to Spurgeon's ministry. Spurgeon's gospel was 'contradictory'. He taught

[1] *Earthen Vessel*, 1857, p. 32.

[58]

human sinfulness but by calling his hearers indiscriminately to faith in Christ ('duty-faith'), he was preaching a
doctrine of works, for dead, captive sinners cannot exercise
faith:

'There is no doctrine in existence that more *insidiously*
destroys the vital truths of the gospel from the churches
than this duty-faith doctrine. It is by this doctrine that such
numbers are converted – *Such a conversion as it is* … It is
very unpleasant to me to make these almost personal
allusions to Mr Spurgeon … I know no man I should feel
more attachment to, were he but straight in the truth; but it
is not so; I lament it; and none but the Lord can alter it.'[1]

In his next issue, under the heading, 'Mr James Wells
and Mr Spurgeon,' Banks complained of 'a most difficult
task for us to select from the many letters on this subject.'
He was anxious that readers who 'think Mr Wells stands as
an *enemy* to Mr Spurgeon' should know 'It is NOT so.' In
the correspondence from which Banks proceeded to give
selections about equal space was given to both sides.

In the July 1857 issue, this correspondence was followed up at length by Wells himself, who set himself the
not difficult task of proving that Spurgeon was a 'duty-
faith' preacher from his published sermons. Among the
statements of Spurgeon to which he objected was the
following: '"I am afraid I am not elect." Oh! dear souls, do
not trouble yourselves about that; if you believe in your
Christ you are elect; whosoever puts himself on the mercy
of Jesus, and who has nothing at all tonight, shall have
mercy if he come for it.'

'What am I to understand by this?' asked Wells. 'Do not

[1] *Earthen Vessel*, 1857, p. 110.

such words quietly set election aside, and rest the whole matter with the creature ... this mode of address to my mind is like having more faith in the supposed power of the creature than in the truth of the living God.'[1]

It was not until the September 1857 issue that Banks could take up the considerable correspondence which arrived on his desk in protest against what Wells had written on Spurgeon. He published only one such letter. Its writer complained that the effect of Wells' words upon those who had not heard Spurgeon 'was to prejudice them very strongly against him', and went on: 'Mr Wells is a good preacher, but I am sure he is wrong respecting Mr Spurgeon. I heard Mr Spurgeon twice last Tuesday at Wellingborough, and I am prepared to tell Mr Wells that two sermons more full of gospel truth, or more free from "deceitful rhetoric", I never heard, either *in* London or *out* of it.'

Some unpublished letters were clearly less moderate. At least one, as quoted by Banks, called the *Earthen Vessel* 'the tool of Mr Wells'. To all these correspondents Banks replied at length. He confessed that he 'sometimes wished that he [Wells] could have written otherwise than he has done', but he was certain of the esteem that the long-time pastor of Surrey Tabernacle deserved from Christians and he believed that, 'In trying and testing Mr Spurgeon's ministry, Mr Wells has aimed at the good of Zion.'[2] Banks clearly felt the difficulty of his position both as a Christian and as a pastor among churches where duty-faith had long

---

[1] *Earthen Vessel*, 1857, p. 155. The quotation is from a sermon on 'Future Bliss'.

[2] *Earthen Vessel*, 1857, pp. 198-9.

been regarded by most as an error. As already said, on that point of doctrine he agreed with Wells and he was only acting according to his own convictions when in that same issue of September 1857 he published a contribution from another pastor which set out to prove three things:

'1. Duty-faith dishonours God. To preach that it is man's duty to believe savingly in Christ is absurd. A babe in grace knows better … 2. Duty-faith points the sinner to himself for a remedy against sin … 3. Duty-faith is calculated to mislead and deceive.'[1]

But, at the same time, Banks refused to support Wells' assessment of Spurgeon. While he rejected the attitude displayed to Wells by some of his correspondents, he repeated the words of commendation which he had written on Spurgeon in 1854 and believed that he was in a better position to judge his ministry than was the pastor of Surrey Tabernacle. Banks told his readers that he had been at Spurgeon's bedside when he was ill, and he had also heard him 'contend for the distinguishing doctrines of grace most vehemently and comprehensively … In these things, perhaps, we have an advantage over Mr Wells, who has, we believe, never either seen or heard Mr Spurgeon.'[2]

After this, controversy died down for a while. In the summer of 1858 a rumour circulated that Wells had changed his mind and had asked Spurgeon to preach for him. A delighted reader wrote to the *Earthen Vessel:* 'I rejoice in seeing that Mr Wells is taking a different view… It seems Mr Editor, that you were right, and Mr Wells wrong, in your first opinions of the pastor of New Park

[1] *Earthen Vessel,* 1857, p. 208.    [2] *Earthen Vessel,* 1857, p. 199.

Street.' The rumour, however, was only a rumour and, as events proved, Banks was right to be doubtful of it in an editorial comment. By now, it seems, he had given up any hope of seeing Spurgeon within their ranks: 'From the first, we believe, Mr Spurgeon determined not to be identified with any party; or to be strictly associated with any of the leaders of any of the existing denominations. He knew that in *some* things he differed from the *whole* of them.'[1]

Towards the end of 1859 the controversy revived and broadened, occasioned again by the pen of Wells. He had previously accused Spurgeon of possessing unsatisfactory views of divine sovereignty and he now took up the whole subject of sovereignty in a series of letters in the *Earthen Vessel*. What he wrote produced a strong protest which Banks published in the December 1859 issue. The writer of this protest complained that Wells was minimising the love of God, and that he was guilty of 'a great mistake' in teaching that God has a hatred for sinners which is both eternal and 'purely' sovereign. In commenting on this protest, Banks agreed that Wells 'has astonished many' by his statements and went on: 'We have thought that his words did not convey his meaning; or, that the thoughts of his mind were not fully or clearly developed. We are waiting for him to conclude his Letters on this, the highest branch of heavenly theology.'

A number of Banks' readers were clearly not prepared to wait. Such was 'the heavy tide of correspondence' which the editor now received that he took the unprecedented step of adding Supplements to the January and February issues of 1860. A senior Particular Baptist pastor, George

[1] *Earthen Vessel,* 1858, p. 179.

Wyard of Deptford, wrote to reprobate Wells' statement 'that God hates without fault', i.e., fault on the part of man, and he illustrated what such a belief can lead to from the case he had heard of a 'young blustering minister' who told his hearers: 'I believe that God does hate some of you and that He always will! do what you will He will hate you, whether you believe or not – whether you pray or not – whether you repent or not – God hates you and will hate you!'

Wyard went on to ask: 'O sir, would it not have been more like a Gospel preacher to have proclaimed after the Master, "Him that cometh unto me I will in no wise cast out;" or after the Apostle, "Be it known unto you, that through this man is preached unto you the forgiveness of sins: and that by him ALL that believe are justified from all things" etc.'[1]

Both sides were given space in the February issue and Spurgeon's name was directly introduced in a long contribution entitled 'Mr Spurgeon's Views of Responsibility and Sovereignty'. The writer of this article had read Spurgeon's sermon, 'God's Sovereignty and Man's Responsibility' and was thoroughly hostile to what he had read. He was shocked that Spurgeon could find fault with William Huntington's views of human responsibility, and still more shocked that Spurgeon apparently believed that God desired the salvation of all who hear the gospel. 'Mr Spurgeon says that God stretched out his arms daily to save them (the Jews), and yet he didn't save them; which I say is positive proof in itself, that he did not stretch out his arms to save them.'[2] The writer was certain that Spurgeon

---

[1] *Earthen Vessel,* 1860, p. 28.     [2] *Earthen Vessel,* 1860, p. 58.

left his hearers 'in as dense a fog with regard to the doctrine of responsibility as they were before.'

The controversy was now at its height. One of Banks' contributors believed: 'There is a sort of Hyper-Calvinism in many of our churches which cannot be made to square with the Scriptures ... It is no longer old fashioned Calvinism, but a stage higher, and another upon that, making it super-hyper, and here and there even this is running to seed.'[1] The subject spilled over into the other Particular Baptist magazines. The Editors of the *Gospel Herald* believed there was indeed cause for concern. They observed a 'monstrous perversion of Divine sovereignty and dominion, the influence of which appears to be widely extending.'[2] The *Gospel Standard* and *Zion's Witness* appeared to have no such fears. The editor of the *Gospel Standard,* J. C. Philpot, was asked by one of his readers whether, in the absence of 'orthodox' preaching, it was 'better to go to a church or chapel in which it is contended that it is the duty of all men to believe unto salvation' or 'to stay at home?' He replied, 'Better far to stay at home, with his Bible, Hart's hymns, and the writings of good men, than to be found in the congregation of the dead.'[3] *Zion's*

[1] *Earthen Vessel,* 1860, p. 312.

[2] *Gospel Herald,* November 1859, p. iv. The *Herald* did not share in the criticism of Spurgeon: 'We have no sympathy with those who would detract from the fame of the youthful pastor of Park Street. We rather rejoice that God has raised him up' (1858, p. 136). In a review of a sermon by Wells on divine sovereignty, the *Herald* said: 'It is seldom we have read a discourse with more pain, and so antagonistic do we deem it to all right views of the character and moral government of God, that we feel it our duty to guard our readers against the influence which the notoriety it has gained may exercise' (1859, p. 124).

[3] *Gospel Standard,* 1861, p. 383.

*Witness* was likewise so extreme in some of its views that one correspondent in the *Earthen Vessel* described it as 'Calvinism run mad'.[1]

Banks had no heart for controversy of this kind and, after thousands of words had been expended, he abandoned any further attempt to reach more unity among the churches which he loved. Doctrinal debate was not where his strength lay and he wanted to embrace all who belonged to his Saviour. He regretted, as he wrote in 1863, that some people believed Mr Wells to be 'a hyper-critical hyper of all hypers',[2] but his magazine had scarcely helped to disabuse anyone of that opinion. Probably by that date there was no need for him to defend Wells' character in his columns for, despite the measure of openness, the *Vessel* had clearly sided against 'duty-faith' and the number of his readers who stood with Spurgeon must have fallen off. Medhurst, for instance, had become a contributor to the *Gospel Herald.* Yet some among Banks' readers evidently continued to regard invitations addressed to the unconverted as true gospel preaching. When an article by a B. B. Wale on 'Ministerial "Appeals to the Unconverted"' appeared in 1864, with special criticism of Spurgeon, it received a very effective reply from a J. E. Cracknell, entitled, 'Calvinism and Hyper-Calvinism'. This led to further material being published from the two men, with by far the greater space taken by Wale. Cracknell had soon concluded that further debate was useless. Minds were made up. Wale believed that of Wells' judgment of Spurgeon, first expressed in his letter to the *Earthen Vessel* in January 1855, 'Every word in that letter has come true.'[3]

[1] *Earthen Vessel,* 1860, p. 309.
[2] *Earthen Vessel,* 1863, p. 217.    [3] *Earthen Vessel,* 1863, p. 231.

# 5

## *Spurgeon's Fourfold Appeal to Scripture*

Through the whole time that controversy on Hyper-Calvinism raged in the *Earthen Vessel*, Spurgeon took no direct part in it even though he was in a real sense its cause. Although we know that he read Banks' monthly, he contributed nothing to its columns. But this is not to say he was silent on the subject, far from it. He chose rather to make his mind known in his printed sermons, published weekly at one penny, and with a circulation of 20,000 by the 1860s.

If expediency had influenced Spurgeon's judgment there were good reasons why he might have said nothing on the controversy which Wells had raised. He was, after all, in the pastorate of Dr Gill and to criticise Hyper-Calvinism would be to risk alienating some of his own people who looked back with veneration on all the history of their congregation and on their famous minister. Further, Spurgeon was already heavily committed on one controversial front without facing another. His assault on the Arminianism which was popular in large sections of English evangelicalism had left him with few ministerial supporters,[1] and many of his most likely allies in that

[1] I have documented this at length in *The Forgotten Spurgeon*. That

controversy would be among the Particular Baptists. To contend simultaneously against Hyper-Calvinism would be to lose sympathy in that quarter for he knew that a considerable section of the Particular and Strict Baptists regarded the teaching of such men as James Wells as the purest orthodoxy. Even in Spurgeon's very first year in London, before any controversy on the issue had become public, he had found himself excluded from one Baptist chapel 'because,' in his own words, 'I was too low in doctrine for the Hyper-Calvinist friends.'[1]

As Spurgeon wrote to his father in the letter already quoted, he had already opposed Hyper-Calvinism in his first pastorate at Waterbeach, but a country chapel in Cambridgeshire was a different proposition from South London where the teaching had long been held among Baptist and Independent churches. Hyper-Calvinists asserted the facts of the gospel, they taught that eternal life is the gift of God, bestowed solely on account of the work of Jesus Christ, and they upheld the supernaturalism of grace. Was this not enough to ensure co-operation in the service of Christ? Spurgeon did not hesitate in believing that it was not and, far from his attitude being due to a weakening in his Calvinism, it was his very concern that true Calvinism should be recovered that led him to give unqualified rejection to Hyper-Calvinism. He believed that the influence of the latter, especially in its worst

---

it was his *primary* controversy should not be forgotten: 'Free grace in its discrimination and omnipotence is not yet preached by the mass of our ministers' (*NPSP*, vol. 3, p. vi, and innumerable similar references).

[1] *Autobiography*, vol. 2, pp. 82–3.

forms,[1] had done untold damage among the Baptist churches. His view was unquestionably the same as that of J. W. Morris, a Baptist minister of an earlier generation and Fuller's biographer, who, speaking of the men whose theology had misdirected the eighteenth-century Baptists, wrote: 'By stretching what are usually called the doctrines of grace, beyond the scripture medium, they introduced a system of *Hyper-Calvinism,* which extended its baleful influence over nearly all the churches, and covered them with a cloud of darkness.'[2] This is precisely what Spurgeon was referring to when, at the laying of the foundation stone of the Metropolitan Tabernacle in 1859, he declared: 'The stone has to be rolled away from the sepulchre of Calvinism yet. The Calvinism of some men is not the Calvinism of John Calvin, nor the Calvinism of the Puritans, much less the Christianity of God.'[3] And elsewhere: 'There are some

---

[1] A number of Hyper-Calvinist preachers were 'theoretical Antinomians' (*anti-nomos,* literally, 'against law'), that is to say, while teaching that the ten commandments are not a rule of life for believers, in practice they upheld the commandments in their personal lives. But, working out the tendency of their teaching, some of their hearers did not live such attractive lives and gave some justice to the accusation that 'Calvinism' (i.e., Hyper-Calvinism) ran counter to godliness: 'Better for you, though it were one of the worst things that could be, if you were to endorse Arminianism rather than Antinomianism. Of the two devils I think the white devil is the least devilish ... Have nothing to do with that horrible spirit which has done more to destroy sound doctrine in our churches than anything else. Arguments will never break Antinomianism down' (*NPSP*, vol. 6, pp. 298–9). As John Duncan once shrewdly observed, 'Every unconverted Arminian is a Pelagian and every unconverted Calvinist is an Antinomian'. Further on this subject see below, pp. 155–7.

[2] *Memoirs of Fuller,* p. 265.

[3] *NPSP,* vol. 5, pp. 367–8.

men who preach this doctrine who are doing ten thousand times more harm than good.'[1] He was concerned that people should know that what Wells and others called 'Calvinism' was not what he regarded as orthodox Christianity. For him the matter was indeed serious enough to warrant controversy and there were four major reasons why he opposed the error as he did. To these we will now turn.

### Gospel Invitations are Universal

Spurgeon believed that historic evangelicalism differed from Hyper-Calvinism over the persons to whom the promises of the gospel are to be preached. Hyper-Calvinism views gospel preaching solely as a means for the ingathering of God's elect. It argues that such words as, 'Trust in Christ and you will be saved', should only be addressed to elect sinners for it is their salvation alone which the preacher should have in view. For a preacher to convey to his hearers the impression that they are all called to receive Christ, and to believe in him for salvation, is to deny, in the opinion of Hyper-Calvinists, the sovereignty of divine grace. It is to represent salvation as available to those whom God has excluded by the decree of election. Gospel preaching for Hyper-Calvinists means a declaration of the facts of the gospel but nothing should be said by way of encouraging individuals to believe that the promises of Christ are made to them particularly until there is evidence that the Spirit of God has begun a saving work in their hearts, convicting them and making them 'sensible' of their need.

[1] *NPSP*, vol. 4, p. 341.

Spurgeon rejected the placing of such a restriction upon the invitation of the gospel. The gospel is 'good news' which God would have proclaimed throughout the world and to 'every creature'. Its message is not simply a statement of facts. It also contains clear, unrestricted general promises, such as, 'He that believeth on him is not condemned' (*John* 3:18); 'Whosoever shall call on the name of the Lord shall be saved' (*Rom.* 10:13); 'Whosoever will, let him take the water of life freely' (*Rev.* 22:17). So the preacher has not done his work when he has spoken of Christ and proclaimed the historic facts of salvation. From there he must go on to urge the reception of Christ upon all men. In the name of God he must assure all of the certainty of their welcome and forgiveness on their repentance and faith. Thus Paul said to all his hearers at Antioch in Pisidia: 'Be it known unto you, men and brethren, that through this man is preached unto you the forgiveness of sins: And by him all that believe are justified from all things, from which ye could not be justified by the law of Moses' (*Acts* 13:38-9). The apostle evidently knew of no limitations. Christ was to be preached, 'warning every man' – any one, every one – 'and teaching every man in all wisdom; that we may present every man perfect in Christ Jesus' (*Col.* 1:28). Words could scarcely be more embracing and individual.

Hyper-Calvinists argued that gospel promises and invitations cannot be made universal because saving grace is special and particular. Spurgeon replied by asserting that the language of Scripture can be given no other meaning. In a sermon entitled 'Apostolic Exhortation', on Peter's words to all his hearers, 'Repent ye therefore and be converted, that your sins may be blotted out' (*Acts* 3:19), he says:

'Peter preached the Christ of the gospel – preached it personally and directly at the crowd who were gathered around him ... Grown up among us is a school of men who say that they rightly preach the gospel to sinners when they merely deliver statements of what the gospel is, and the result of dying unsaved, but they grow furious and talk of unsoundness if any venture to say to the sinner, "Believe", or "Repent". To this school Peter did not belong – into their secret he had never come, and with their assembly, were he alive now, he would not be joined.'[1]

In another sermon he refers to brethren who 'do not think it to be their duty to go into the highways and hedges and bid all, as many as they find, to come to the supper. Oh, no! They are too orthodox to obey the Master's will; they desire to understand first who are appointed to come to the supper, and then they will invite them; that is to say, they will do what there is no necessity to do [i.e., present the gospel to those who are already saved].'

In contrast with this, the apostles 'delivered *the* gospel, the same gospel to the dead as to the living, the same gospel to the non-elect as to the elect. The point of distinction is not in the gospel, but in its being applied by the Holy Ghost, or left to be rejected of man.'[2]

### The Warrant of Faith

A second reason why Spurgeon rejected Hyper-Calvinism was that it turned individuals away from their only sure warrant for trusting in Christ, namely, the objective

[1] *MTP,* vol. 14, p. 194.

[2] *MTP,* vol. 11, p. 495. There are many similar statements in his early sermons, e.g., *MTP,* vol. 8, pp. 199, 554.

commands and invitations of the gospel. Hyper-Calvinism denies such a universal warrant, applicable to all, and claims, instead, that Scripture only addresses invitations to specific people – to the penitent, the 'heavy laden', to the convicted, to the 'sensible' sinner and so on. Under such preaching, gospel hearers must first find some warrant within themselves for thinking that Christ's invitations are addressed to them personally. Subjective experience is thus made a kind of necessary preliminary and qualification before anyone can trust in scriptural promises.[1] Against this, Spurgeon held that the scriptural warrant for the unconverted to trust in Christ rests on nothing in

[1] That a work of God in the heart is necessary in order that a sinner comes to faith Spurgeon never doubted, on the contrary he preached it clearly but it is not with *that* work that the sinner is to be concerned; his attention is to be fixed upon the warrant. God has much to do in us but requires nothing *of us* before we come to Christ. The *way* to faith and the *warrant* of faith are not the same things. Sinners, says Owen, 'are not directed first to secure their souls that they are born again, and then afterwards to believe; but they are first to believe that the remission of sin is tendered to them in the blood of Christ ... nor is it the duty of men to question whether they have faith or no, but actually to believe; and faith in its operation will evidence itself' (*Works of John Owen*, vol. 6, p. 598). God works in the heart and *with* the promises, and to treat the inward work of God as though it were over against the duty of believing the promises, as Hyper-Calvinism generally does, is to cause confusion for seeking souls. This confusion can be seen in the words of Joseph Hussey, one of the first Hyper-Calvinists, who declared: 'We ought to declare the gospel in the encouragements of it unto salvation. But offers [i.e. general invitations, promising salvation to all who repent and believe] are no encouragements to salvation ... Encouragements are the operations of his grace.' Quoted by Peter Toon, *The Emergence of Hyper-Calvinism in English Non-Conformity 1689–1765* (London: The Olive Tree, 1967), p. 82. Further on this point, see below, pp. 140–2.

themselves; the warrant lies in the invitation of Christ. His entire presentation of the gospel turned on the truth that no sinner has any more warrant than any other for trusting in Christ. The warrant lies in Scripture alone. Before a man has any willingness to be saved, it is 'his duty to believe in Christ, for it is not man's willingness that gives him a right to believe. Men are to believe in obedience to God's command. God commandeth all men everywhere to repent, and this is his great command, "Believe in the Lord Jesus Christ and thou shalt be saved".'[1] Christ's ambassadors are authorised to call 'on all people of every clime and kindred, to believe the gospel with a promise of personal salvation to each and every one that believes.'[2] The message is not, 'Wait for feelings', it is, 'Believe and live'. 'I find Jesus Christ says nothing to sinners about waiting, but very much about coming.'[3]

To this the Hyper-Calvinists replied that if all are called to trust in Christ then such trust must involve them in believing a falsehood because Christ has not died for all. In their view, to preach a universal warrant is to deny that redemption is definite and particular. This was a further ground for charging Spurgeon with inconsistency, for he believed in particular redemption and yet summoned all to believe in Christ.[4] But Spurgeon, along with Scripture, did not make, 'Believe that Christ died for you', part of faith to which the unbeliever is summoned. The call to the sinner is to commit himself to Christ, *not* because he has been saved but rather because he is lost and must come to

[1] *MTP,* vol. 7, p. 191.
[2] *MTP,* vol. 15, p. 626.     [3] *MTP,* vol. 13, p. 196.
[4] The reason Spurgeon did not believe in universal redemption is summarised in my *Forgotten Spurgeon,* 1973, pp. 73–8.

Jesus in order to be saved. Hyper-Calvinism errs with Arminianism in thinking that a knowledge of the *extent* of the atonement is necessary if true faith is to be exercised. But that is not the case. As John Rippon wrote when he disagreed with Gill on saving faith:

'To believe in Christ, is not for the sinner to assure himself that Christ died for him in particular, which every Arminian who maintains *universal* redemption must certainly do, though multitudes of such give demonstrable evidence that they have not the faith connected with salvation; but "to believe in him", is to give such a practical credit to the scriptural testimony concerning Christ as is connected with our personal application to him that he may save us.'[1]

This still does not answer the question, How can sinners be offered a salvation which Christ did not fulfil on their behalf? Spurgeon set that question aside as something which God has not chosen to explain.[2] It was enough for

[1] *Brief Memoir of the Life and Writings of Gill* (1811; repr. Harrisonburg, Va.: Gano Books, 1992), p. 44. Further on this point see *Redemption: Accomplished and Applied*, John Murray (Banner of Truth, 1979), p. 65.

[2] He would have agreed heartily with the words of Robert M'Cheyne Edgar writing on 'Recent Attacks on Calvinism' in the *British and Foreign Evangelical Review* (London: James Nisbet, 1881), p. 417: 'There are two positions possible upon this subject: first, we may declare it impossible for God to be sincere in His general offer, if His atonement be limited in its extent; or, secondly, we may believe it possible for the Almighty to reconcile a limited atonement with a general offer, and that He will do so in His own good time, while our duty meanwhile is to proclaim the gospel fully and freely upon the ground of this assurance. The latter is the Calvinistic position. It is the attitude of trust. It is the resolve to walk by faith, and not by sight, in this high mystery. The advocates of a universal atonement, on the other

him to know that Christ does offer himself to all; that the gospel is for 'every creature', that all who come to him will be saved, and that all who reject him will be without excuse. A universal proclamation of good news, with a warrant for every creature, lay at the heart of his understanding of Scripture. To 'the rulers of Sodom', for example, in Isaiah 1:18, God says: 'Come now, and let us reason together ... though your sins be as scarlet, they shall be as white as snow.' 'These were men,' says Spurgeon, 'whose very religion was hateful to God,' yet it is such that God invites to receive mercy, just as the crucifiers of Christ were later to be invited on the day of Pentecost. So urging the same point from the New Testament, Spurgeon goes on:

' "Repent and be baptized every one of you", said Peter. As John Bunyan puts it – one man might have stood up in the crowd and said, "But I helped to hound him to the cross!" "Repent and be baptized *every one of you.*" "But I drove the nails into his hands!" saith one. "*Every one of you*", says Peter. "But I pierced his side." "*Every one of you*", said Peter. "And I put my tongue into my cheek and stared at his nakedness and said, 'If he be the Son of God, let him come down from the cross!' " "*Every one of you*",

----

hand, refuse to give God credit for the ability to make the reconciliation between the definite and limited atonement and the general offer of His gospel. They seem to think that the skein becomes too tangled for the Divine fingers, that the general proclamation may be so accepted as to upset the definite purposes of the Most High, that, in a word, the Omniscience and Omnipotence of God are insufficient as a guarantee against a collision between the electing decree and the general offer of the gospel.'

said Peter. "Repent and be baptized every one of you." I do feel so grieved at many of our Calvinistic brethren; they know nothing about Calvinism I am sorry to say, for never was any man more caricatured by his professed followers than John Calvin. Many of them are afraid to preach from Peter's text ... When I do it, they say, "He is unsound". But I do not care for that; I know the Lord has blessed my appeals to all sorts of sinners, and none shall stay me in giving free invitations as long as I find them in this Book.'[1]

In addition to the biblical case that gospel invitations are not to be limited to those possessing certain experiences, Spurgeon added the argument that such a limitation is bound to confuse needy souls and to endanger them with a form of legality. He treats this subject fully in a sermon entitled 'The Warrant of Faith' from 1 John 3:23, 'And this is his commandment that we should believe on the name of his Son Jesus Christ':

'In our own day certain preachers assure us that a man must be regenerated before we may bid him believe in Jesus Christ; some degree of a work of grace in the heart being, in their judgment, the only warrant to believe. This also is false. It takes away a gospel for sinners and offers us a gospel for saints ... Brethren, the command to believe in Christ must be the sinner's warrant, if you consider the nature of our commission. How runs it? "Go ye into all the world, and preach the gospel to every creature." It ought to read, according to the other plan, "preach the gospel to every regenerate person, to every convinced sinner, to every sensible sinner." But it is not so; it is to "every creature".'

---

[1] *MTP*, vol. 7, pp. 148–9.

To deny a universal warrant, and to require subjective experiences before Christ is trusted, is bound to lead to confusion and legality. Such teaching makes men look at themselves instead of the Saviour. It leads people to suppose that possessing a broken heart and feeling the burden of sin are some kind of qualification for believing. But this is to require a discernment on the part of would-be converts for which Scripture does not ask. The truth is that individuals under conviction are unable to understand themselves and it is common for those who are most burdened to fear that they have no true sense of sin at all. The Holy Spirit is indeed given to convict of sin but Scripture says nothing about him assuring the convicted of their convictions prior to faith. On this Spurgeon says in the same sermon on 'The Warrant of Faith':

'I believe the tendency of that preaching which puts the warrant for faith anywhere but in the gospel command, is to vex the true penitent, and to console the hypocrite; the tendency of it is to make the poor soul which really repents, feel that he must not believe in Christ, because he sees so much of his own hardness of heart. The more spiritual a man is, the more unspiritual he see himself to be ... Often the most penitent men are those who think themselves the most impenitent.'[1]

---

[1] *MTP*, vol. 9, p. 537. 'All this preaching to sinners that they must feel this and feel that before they trust in Jesus, is just self-righteousness in another shape ... Phariseeism is mixed with Hyper-Calvinism more than with any other sect in the world.' *NPSP*, vol. 6, p. 403. 'What God gives us on the account of sanctification, we are ready enough to reckon on the score of justification. It is a hard thing to feel grace, and to believe as if there were none. We have so much of the Pharisee in us by nature' (*Works of Owen*, vol. 6, p. 600).

'If we begin to preach to sinners that they must have a certain sense of sin and a certain measure of conviction, *such teaching would turn the sinner away from God in Christ to himself.* The man begins at once to say, "Have I a broken heart? Do I feel the burden of sin?" This is only another form of looking at self. Man must not look to himself to find reasons for God's grace.'[1]

Spurgeon's own experience under conviction, as well as that of others, confirmed him in this judgment:

'When I read, "Come unto Me, all ye that labour and are heavy laden, and I will give you rest;" I said, "That belongs to my brother, to my sister," or those around me; for they were all "heavy laden," I thought, but I was not; and though, God knoweth, I would weep, and cry, and lament till my heart was breaking within me, if any man had asked me whether I sorrowed for sin, I should have told him, "No, I have never had any true sorrow for sin." "Well, do you not feel the burden of sin?" "No!" "But you really are a convinced sinner?" "No," I should have said, "I am not." '[2]

The only antidote to this condition is for sinners to understand the absolute freeness and universality of the gospel invitation:

[1] *MTP*, vol. 33, pp. 114–5. 'You may keep your visions, and ecstasies, and raptures, and dancings to yourselves; the only feeling that I desire to have is deep repentance and humble faith' (*NPSP*, vol. 3, p. 270). An intensely subjective interest in 'experience' in conversion has generally prevailed in Hyper-Calvinistic churches, a condition not helped by the fact that the testimonies of their preachers, such as Huntington and Wells, have commonly been highly dramatic. For Huntington, see *The Kingdom of Heaven Taken by Prayer* in *Select Works of W. Huntington* (Bennett: London, 1837), and for Wells, *Memoirs of James Wells*, W. Crowther, 1873.

[2] *Autobiography*, vol. 1, p. 86.

'The gospel is that you believe in Christ Jesus; that you get right out of yourself, and depend alone in him. Do you say, "I feel so guilty"? You are certainly guilty, whether you feel it or not; you are far more guilty than you have any idea of. Come to Christ because you are guilty, not because you have been prepared to come by looking at your guilt. Trust nothing of your own, not even your sense of need.'[1]

'Sinners, let me address you with words of life; Jesus wants nothing from you, nothing whatsoever, nothing done, nothing felt; he gives both work and feeling. Ragged, penniless, just as you are, lost, forsaken, desolate, with no good feelings, and no good hopes, still Jesus comes to you, and in these words of pity he addresses you, "Him that cometh unto me I will in no wise cast out"'.[2]

'"Him that cometh to me:" … the man may have been guilty of an atrocious sin, too black for mention; but if he comes to Christ he shall not be cast out. He may have made himself as black as night – as black as hell … I cannot tell what kind of persons may have come into this Hall to-night; but if burglars, murderers, and dynamite-men were here, I would still bid them come to Christ, for he will not cast them out. No limit is set to the extent of sin: any "him" in all the world – any blaspheming, devilish "him" that comes to Christ shall be welcomed. I use strong words that I may open the gate of mercy. Any "him" that comes to Christ – though he come from slum or taproom, betting-ring or gambling-hell, prison or brothel – Jesus will in no wise cast out.'[3]

---

[1] *MTP*, vol. 33, p. 115.      [2] *MTP*, vol. 9, pp. 537–8.
[3] *MTP*, vol. 30, pp. 54–5.

Spurgeon spoke in this way because he knew that the Spirit of God does not supersede man's moral faculties in conversion but works in them and through them by the truth. He would have agreed entirely with the words of T. J. Crawford: 'The promise of divine power to quicken those souls which are "dead in trespasses and sins", can be warrantably pleaded and hopefully relied on *in connection with the fully issued call of the Gospel and with that alone. If the call be materially qualified and restricted, so as to come far short of the full requirements of the Gospel,* we have no ground to think that it will be accompanied with the life-giving power and energy of the Holy Spirit.'[1]

**Human Responsibility**
The two convictions so far stated – that gospel invitations are to be addressed to all, and that the warrant to believe lies in the commands and promises of Scripture – lead us to the heart of the dispute between evangelical Calvinism and Hyper-Calvinism. It concerns the place of man's responsibility or, to use an equivalent term, his free-agency. Terminology here is important. Free-agency is not to be confused with 'free-will'. Since the Fall, men have not lost their responsibility but they have lost the ability, the will, to obey God. Thus Spurgeon could say, 'I dread more than anything your being left to your own free-will'. Hyper-Calvinism argues that sinners cannot be required to do what they are not able to do, namely, to believe in Christ for salvation. The ability to believe belongs only to the elect, and that at the time determined by the Spirit of God.

---

[1] T. J. Crawford, *The Mysteries of Christianity* (Edinburgh: Blackwoods, 1874), p. 285.

So for a preacher to call all his hearers to immediate repentance and faith is to deny both human depravity and the sovereignty of grace.

Spurgeon did not reply to this argument, as many have done, by weakening the biblical teaching on human depravity and inability. His sermons prove the truth of his words, 'We shall proclaim the doctrine of God's sovereignty, without toning it down, and electing love without stuttering over it.'[1] He asserted, as strongly as it has ever been asserted, that the will of God is omnipotent both in the provision and in the application of every part of salvation: 'Our Lord's mission was not so much to save all whom he addressed, as to save out of them as many as his Father gave him.'[2] But his response to the Hyper-Calvinist argument was to assert another equally biblical truth, namely, that man is wholly responsible for his own sin. God is not its author. Those who hear the gospel and reject the Saviour will not be able to plead that sovereignty prevented them from exercising the obedience of faith. None will be able to claim that God excluded them. No, it is on account of sin alone, including the sin of unbelief, that unrepentant sinners will finally be condemned and lost for ever.

Asked to explain such a mystery, Spurgeon constantly

---

[1] *Only a Prayer-Meeting,* p. 304. The quotation is from a chapter on 'Preaching to Sinners' in which he says some gospel preaching is like a school-boy he heard of who would toss a luscious apple before his friend's eyes but then put it back in his pocket. 'When I am preaching to sinners, I feel inclined always to beg every one of them to put the golden apple in his pocket, for this choice fruit of life may belong to millions, and yet the whole of it will remain for millions more.'

[2] *MTP,* vol. 19, p. 277.

replied that it was not his business to do so. His duty was to deal with the whole range of scriptural truth and to declare it in its true proportions. To limit the message to such truths as we can see to be consistent with each other is to exercise a liberty to which we have no right. The great error of Hyper-Calvinism is to neglect one side of the Word of God because it does not know how to explain both that the will of God is effective and sovereign in all things *and* that man is free and responsible for all his actions. 'Both are true; no two truths can be inconsistent with each other; and what you have to do is to believe them both.'[1] In an early sermon on 'Sovereign Grace and Man's Responsibility' Spurgeon introduced his subject with these words:

'The system of truth is not one straight line, but two. No man will ever get a right view of the gospel until he knows how to look at the two lines at once ... Now, if I were to declare that man was so free to act, that there is no presidence of God over his actions, I should be driven very near to atheism; and if, on the other hand, I declare that God so overrules all things, as that man is not free to be responsible, I am driven at once to Antinomianism or fatalism. That God predestinates, and that man is responsible, are two things that few can see. They are believed to be inconsistent and contradictory; but they are not. It is the fault of our weak judgment ... it is my folly that leads me to imagine that two truths can ever contradict each other.'[2]

This emphasis will be found over and over again in his sermons. Let me give two more extracts:

'I believe in predestination, yea, even in its very jots and tittles. I believe that the path of a single grain of dust in the

[1] *NPSP,* vol. 4, p. 343.    [2] *NPSP,* vol. 4, p. 337.

March wind is ordained and settled by a decree which cannot be violated; that every word and thought of man, every flittering of a sparrow's wing, every flight of a fly ... that everything, in fact is foreknown and foreordained. But I do equally believe in the free agency of man, that man acts as he wills, especially in moral operations – choosing the evil with a will that is unbiased by anything that comes from God, biased only by his own depravity of heart and the perverseness of his habits; choosing the right too, with perfect freedom, though sacredly guided and led by the Holy Spirit ... I believe that man is as accountable as if there were no destiny whatever ... Where these two truths meet I do not know, nor do I want to know. They do not puzzle me, since I have given up my mind to believing them both.'[1]

Elsewhere on the same theme he says:

'Some have supposed that when we believe with David, in Psalm 115, that God hath done whatsoever he hath pleased, we deny free agency, and of necessity moral responsibility also. Nay, but we declare that those who would do so are tinctured with the old captious spirit of him who said, "Why doth he yet find fault, for who hath resisted his will?" and our answer is that of Paul, "Nay, but O man, who art thou that repliest against God?" Can you understand it, for I cannot, how a man is a free agent, a responsible agent, so that his sin is his own wilful sin and lies with him and never with God, and yet at the same time God's purposes are fulfilled, and his will is done even by demons and corrupt men? – I cannot comprehend it: without hesitation I believe it, and rejoice so to do, I never hope

[1] *MTP,* vol. 15, p. 458.

to comprehend it. I worship a God I never expect to comprehend ... It is my firm belief that everything in heaven, and earth and hell, will be seen to be, in the long run, part of the divine plan; yet never is God the author or the accomplice of sin ... sin rests with man, wholly with man, and yet by some strange overruling force, Godlike and mysterious, like the existence of God, his supreme will is accomplished ... to deny this truth because we cannot understand it, were to shut ourselves out of a great deal of important knowledge.'[1]

Spurgeon regarded an emphasis on man's free-agency as absolutely essential to true evangelism. Because Scripture teaches that conversion is the work of God, Hyper-Calvinism fears to appeal for human action lest it interferes with God. But Scripture also presents conversion as the work of man and recognizes no inconsistency in calling upon men to be reconciled to God.[2] Because it does not recognize

[1] *MTP*, vol. 16, p. 501. In a sermon, 'High Doctrine and Broad Doctrine', he elaborates on the same point from John 6:37. 'Predestinating grace' is 'high doctrine', 'whosoever will may come' is broad. 'These are two great truths; let us carry them both with us, and they will balance each other ... The business of removing religious difficulties is the least remunerative labour under heaven. The truest way is to accept the difficulty wherever you find it in God's word, and to exercise your faith upon it ... They are equally precious portions of one harmonious whole. Let us not quibble over them, or indulge a foolish favouritism for one and a prejudice against the other; but let us receive both with a candid, large-hearted love of the truth, such as children of God should exhibit.' *MTP*, vol. 30, pp. 49–50.

[2] Talking of the mystery of the relation between man's responsibility and the will of God, John Duncan, one of the wisest theologians of the nineteenth century, said: 'That God works half, and man the other half, is false; that God works all, and man does all, is true.' As he says, both Arminianism and Hyper-Calvinism (Antinomianism) fail to

this, Hyper-Calvinism fails to tell the unconverted that it is their fault alone if they remain unsaved under the gospel and that their damnation will be their own work. Not only is faith in Christ a duty, but as Spurgeon often showed from Scripture, a refusal to believe on Christ will be found at last to be a greater offence than the iniquities of Sodom and Gomorrah. 'Is it not the very summit of arrogance and the height of pride for a son of Adam to say, even in his heart, "God, I doubt thy grace; God, I doubt Thy love; God, I doubt Thy power"? I feel that, could we roll all sins into one mass, – could we take murder, blasphemy, lust, adultery, fornication, and everything that is vile, and unite them all into one vast globe of black corruption, – they would not even then equal the sin of unbelief.'[1]

In his autobiography Spurgeon reports how in his early days, before he came to London, he found himself with some ministers and others of Hyper-Calvinistic views 'who were disputing whether it was a sin in men that they did not believe the gospel.' The shock he felt on that occasion was to remain with him all his days: 'Whilst they were discussing, I said, "Gentlemen, am I in the presence of Christians? Are you believers in the Bible or are you not?" They said, "We are Christians, of course." "Then," said I, "does not the Scripture say, 'of sin, because they believe not on Me?' And is it not the damning sin of men, that they do not believe on Christ?"'[2]

---

recognize this. (*Colloquia Peripatetica, Notes of Conversations with John Duncan*, ed. W. Knight [Edinburgh, 1907], pp. 29–30).

[1] *Autobiography*, vol. 1, p. 261.

[2] *Autobiography*, vol. 1, p. 260. He refers to the same experience on other occasions, e.g., *NPSP*, vol. 1, pp. 18–19.

Spurgeon used this incident in the second sermon of the first volume of the *New Park Street Pulpit*, entitled 'The Sin of Unbelief', and, as we have seen, much of the contention of Hyper-Calvinism against his preaching concerned this point. 'I hold,' he says, 'as firmly as any man living, that repentance and conversion are the work of the Holy Spirit, but I would sooner lose this hand, and both, than I would give up preaching that it is the duty of men to repent and believe and that it is the duty of Christian ministers to say to them, "Repent and be converted, that your sins may be blotted out."'[1]

Spurgeon frequently spoke against Hyper-Calvinism in his sermons. He did so at some length in an 'Exposition of the Doctrines of Grace' at the time of the opening of the Metropolitan Tabernacle in 1861 when he forcefully repudiated any idea of fatalism and insisted, 'If he be lost, damnation is all of man; but, if he be saved, still salvation is all of God.' God did not make men to be damned but, as Spurgeon showed from the Westminster Assembly's Larger Catechism, wrath is only inflicted on men on account of sin: 'This is no more than what the Methodist and all other Evangelical bodies acknowledge – that where men perish it is in consequence of their sin.'[2]

In his Preface to the *Metropolitan Tabernacle Pulpit* for 1863 he made what was possibly the last of his open appeals to those whom he describes as 'led captive by ultra-calvinistic theories', calling upon them to 'preach the whole gospel, instead of a part': 'Divine sovereignty is a great and indisputable fact, but human responsibility is quite as indisputable ... Faith is God's gift, but it is also the

---

[1] *MTP*, vol. 14, p. 196.  [2] *MTP,* vol. 7, p. 301.

act of renewed manhood. Damnation is the result of justice, not of arbitrary predestination. O that the time were come when seeming opposites would be received, because faith knows that they are portions of one harmonious whole. Would that an enlarged view of the dispensations of God to man would permit men to be faithful to the human race, and at the same time true to the Sovereign Lord of all.'[1]

In the same volume Spurgeon speaks of the 'religion of a man who preaches divine sovereignty but neglects human responsibility', and says: 'I believe it is a vicious, immoral, and corrupt manner of setting forth doctrine, and cannot be of God.'[2]

What this meant for Spurgeon in practice is best seen when he is not thinking of controversy at all but simply urging men and women to come to Christ. We have already looked at the way he pressed the gospel invitation, assuring all that the mercy of God was certain for everyone who complies. 'Can a sinner be saved when he will to come to Christ? *Yea.'*[3] But the other side of this truth was the terrible guilt of those refusing Christ:

'Unregenerate men cannot and will not believe their God. This is also caused by the love of sin. Those who do not wish to give up their favourite sins pretend the gospel is very difficult to understand, or quite impossible to accept … Do you dare to make the gospel the cause of your ruin? Do you ask pity for yourself, as if you could not help being an enemy of God, and a rejecter of his way of mercy? Do you murmur that you cannot see? Who has closed your

---

[1] *MTP,* vol. 9, pp. vi–ii.     [2] *MTP,* vol. 9, p. 153.
[3] *MTP,* vol. 8, p. 190.

eyes? There are none so blind as those who will not see; your blindness is wilful. You do not understand: do you want to understand? ... If you do not desire to be reconciled to God, is it wonderful that you dream that God is unwilling to be reconciled to you? O soul, I beseech you, do not impugn your damnation to your God, who in infinite goodness has brought his word so very near to you!'[1]

'Oh! the thought above all thought the most deadly. I am lost, lost, lost! And this is the horror of horrors: I have caused myself to be lost; I have put from me the gospel of Christ; I have destroyed myself.'[2]

'Oh, my hearers, Will any man choose for himself to be lost? Will he count himself unworthy of eternal life, and put it from him? If you will be damned you must do it yourselves. Your blood be on your own heads. Go down to the pit if you deliberately choose to do so; but this know, that Christ was preached to you, and you would not have him; you were invited to come to him, but you turned your backs on him; you chose for your selves your own eternal destruction! God grant that you may repent of such a choice, for Christ's sake. Amen.'[3]

These quotations lead us on to the fourth and perhaps the most serious difference of all between evangelical Calvinism and Hyper-Calvinism.

### Hyper-Calvinism and the Love of God

Spurgeon saw that behind the distortion of predestination, and the unwillingness to believe that gospel invitations are

[1] *MTP*, vol. 33, p. 333.    [2] *NPSP*, vol. 4, p. 240.
[3] *MTP*, vol. 27, p. 460.

to be addressed freely to all men, lay a failure to understand what Scripture reveals about the character of God himself. If God has chosen an elect people, then, Hyper-Calvinism argued, he can have no desire for the salvation of any others and to speak as though he had, is to deny the particularity of grace. Of course, Hyper-Calvinists accepted that the gospel be preached to all, but they denied that such preaching was intended to demonstrate any love on the part of God for all, or any invitation to all to receive mercy. On the contrary, they taught that no man has any right to trust in a loving God until he has first some personal evidence that he is one of the chosen.

A sermon of 1858 which Spurgeon preached on 'Sovereign Grace and Man's Responsibility' identified this crucial difference with Hyper-Calvinism. He took for his text the words of God quoted by Paul in Romans 10:20–21, 'I was found of them that sought me not; I was made manifest unto them that asked not after me. But to Israel he saith, all day long I have stretched forth my hands unto a disobedient and gainsaying people.' In such words Spurgeon saw the proof that God can be said to desire the salvation even of those who persist in rejecting him:

'Lost sinners who sit under the sound of the gospel are not lost for the want of the most affectionate invitation. God says he stretches out his hands ... What did he wish them to come for? Why, to be saved. "No," says one, "it was for temporal mercies."[1] Not so, my friend; the verse before is concerning spiritual mercies, and so is this one, for they refer to the same thing. Now, was God sincere in his offer? God forgive the man who dares to say he was not.

[1] See below, pp. 128–9.

God is undoubtedly sincere in every act he did. He sent his prophets, he entreated the people of Israel to lay hold on spiritual things, but they would not, and though he stretched out his hands all the day long, yet they were "a disobedient and gainsaying people" and would not have his love.'[1]

Spurgeon regarded the denial of God's desire for the salvation of all men as no mere theoretical mistake. For it converged with one of the greatest obstacles to faith on the part of the unconverted, that is to say, a wrong view of the character of God. Men 'imagine that God is a severe being, angry and fierce, very easily moved to wrath, but not so easily to be induced to love'. The truth of divine love is the last to enter men's heads. Because Hyper-Calvinism is wrong here it fails to disabuse the minds of fallen men of this error. It does not give men the warning to be found in such evangelical Calvinists as John Owen who counselled, 'Let us not entangle our own spirits by limiting his grace ... We are apt to think that we are very willing to have forgiveness, but that God is unwilling to bestow it.' Scripture, Owen continued, sets forth the contrary in order 'to root out all the secret reserves of unbelief concerning God's willingness to give mercy, grace, and pardon unto sinners ... Therefore, the tendency of our former argument is, not merely to prove that there is forgiveness with God, which we may believe and not be mistaken, but which we ought to

---

[1] *NPSP*, vol. 4, p. 341. As John Murray and Ned B. Stonehouse observe, 'It would appear that the real point in dispute in connection with the free offer of the gospel is whether it can properly be said that God *desires* the salvation of all men.' See 'The Free Offer of the Gospel' in *Collected Writings of John Murray* (Banner of Truth, 1982), vol. 4, pp. 113–32.

believe; it is our duty to do so. We are expressly *commanded* to believe, and that upon the highest promises and under the greatest penalties.'[1]

Referring to the same truth, Spurgeon says:

'We think that ultra-calvinism, which goes vastly beyond the teaching of Christ, or the enlightened ministry of Calvin could warrant, gets some of its support from a wrong view of God. To the ultra-calvinist his absolute sovereignty is delightfully conspicuous. He is awe-stricken with the great and glorious attributes of the Most High. His omnipotence appals him, and his sovereignty astonishes him, and he at once submits as by a stern necessity to the will of God. He, however, too much forgets that God is love. He does not make prominent enough the benevolent character of the Divine Being ... To see the holiness, the

---

[1] *Works of John Owen*, vol. 6, pp. 502–4. See also p. 521 where, concerning sinners' refusals of God's promises, he writes: 'Whatever is pretended, it is will and stubbornness that lie at the bottom of this refusal;' and his *Exposition of Hebrews*, vol. 3, p. 309: 'What greater condescension, love, or grace could be conceived or desired? This is tendered in the gospel, 2 Cor. 5:19. Now, what greater indignity can be offered unto him than to reject his tenders?' As Toon points out, Calvin says the same in commenting on Hosea 13:14: 'God does not here simply promise salvation, but shows that he is indeed ready to save, but that the wickedness of the people was an impediment in the way ... *I will* then *redeem them*, as far as this depends on me. What, then, does stand in the way? Even the hardness of the people ... we may learn from this passage, that when men perish, God still continues like himself, and that neither his power, by which he is mighty to save the world, is extinguished, nor his purpose changed, so as not to be always ready to help; but that the obstinacy of men rejects the grace which has been provided, and which God willingly and bountifully offers'. *Commentaries on the Twelve Minor Prophets* (Calvin Translation Society: repr. Banner of Truth, 1986), vol. 1, pp. 476–7.

love, the justice, the faithfulness, the immutability, the omnipotence, and the sovereignty of God, all shining like a bright corona of eternal and ineffable light, this has never been given perfectly to any human being, and inasmuch as we have not seen all these, as we hope yet to see them, our faulty vision has been the ground of divers mistakes.'[1]

If it were not that 'God is love' his presence could never have become desirable to sinners. The gospel presents love as the attraction. 'God so loved.' 'How excellent is thy loving kindness, O God! *therefore* the children of men put their trust under the shadow of thy wings' (*Psa.* 36:7). In the words of John Duncan: 'Love is the great attraction. Without the sternness of holiness and justice it would be the love of an unholy and unjust God; yet the holiness and justice of God repel the sinner.'[2] It is love that draws, as the record of the four Gospels makes abundantly plain. The voice of Christ among men was the voice of love. What was it that moved him as he saw the multitude but a compassion for all? (*Matt.* 9:36). What but love brought him to weep over lost Jerusalem? (*Luke* 19:41) and to say, 'How often would I have gathered thy children ... and ye would not!' (*Matt.* 23:37). What is clearer in Scripture than the evidence that love can be despised? (*Mark* 10:21–22). The preaching of Christ contained a promise of welcome for all and his whole life revealed him longing for the salvation of men and women. 'None of us,' says Spurgeon, 'loves men as Christ loves them; and if the love of all the tender hearted in the world could run together, they would make but a drop compared with the ocean of the compassion of

[1] *MTP,* vol. 7, p. 370.

[2] *In the Pulpit and at the Communion Table,* J. Duncan, ed. D. Brown (Edinburgh, 1874), p. 47.

Jesus.'[1] 'We say, "Sinner, only trust in Christ." Ah, ye do not know what a great "only" that is. It is a work so great that no man can do it unaided by God … But if anything can call faith into exercise,' he goes on, it is the knowledge 'that Christ is willing to receive thee.'[2] Preaching Christ, for Spurgeon, had to include the urging of this knowledge upon all:

' "If any man thirst, let him come unto me and drink." He invites men to come; he pleads with them to come; and when they will not come he gently upbraids them with such words as these, "Ye will not come unto me that ye might have life" … All our Lord's sermons were so many loving calls to poor aching hearts to come and find what they need in him.'[3] 'Beloved, there is nothing that so delights Jesus Christ as to save sinners … You misjudge him if you think he wants to be argued with and persuaded to have mercy; he gives it as freely as the sun pours forth light.'[4] 'Paul had no stinted Saviour to present to a few, no narrow-hearted Christ to be the head of a clique, but he preached a great Saviour to great masses, a great Saviour to great sinners … My Lord Jesus, by his death, has become immensely rich in pardoning grace – so rich indeed that no guiltiness can possibly transcend the efficacy of his precious blood.'[5]

But it is more than knowledge of the love of God as taught in Scripture which preachers need. They must themselves be possessed by the love of which they speak. Invitations to trust in Christ preached without love are no

---

[1] *MTP*, vol. 33, p. 137. The very titles of Spurgeon's sermons so often convey the same message.

[2] *NPSP*, vol. 4, p. 437.   [3] *MTP*, vol. 14, p. 258.

[4] *MTP*, vol. 14, p. 645.   [5] *MTP*, vol. 13, pp. 210–11.

invitations at all. And a preacher who calls men to faith, uncertain about Christ's desire to save his hearers, will never make an evangelist. Present fellowship with Christ is needed to end such doubt. It is Christ's love, known and felt, which creates the spirit seen in such men as Robert Murray M'Cheyne whose hearers believed that he was 'dying to have them converted'. 'We win by love,' says Spurgeon. 'We win hearts for Jesus by love, by sympathy with their sorrows, by anxiety lest they should perish, by pleading with God for them with all our hearts that they would not be left to die unsaved, by pleading with them for God that, for their own sake, they would seek mercy and find grace.'[1]

Such earnestness in calling men to Christ, as John Owen writes, is but a faint representation of the source from whence the call comes: 'It is God himself who ... invites, exhorts, and persuades you to accept ... And excuse us if we are a little in earnest with you in this matter. Alas! our utmost that we can, by zeal for his glory or compassion unto your souls, raise our thoughts, minds, spirits, words unto, comes infinitely short of his own pressing earnestness herein.'[2]

For Spurgeon there was therefore this fundamental need for preachers to know more communion with Christ him-

---

[1] It is noticeable that it was this very feature which revived so markedly in Carey and his associates. Thus Fuller, in his *Memoirs of Samuel Pearce*, wrote: 'the governing principle in Mr Pearce, beyond all doubt, was *holy love* ... eminent spirituality in a minister is usually attended with eminent usefulness.' (Quoted in Morris, *Memoirs of Fuller*, pp. 80, 82).

[2] *Works of John Owen*, vol. 6 (Banner of Truth, 1966), p. 517. See also Spurgeon on 2 Cor. 5:18–21, 'God beseeching sinners by his Ministers', *MTP*, vol. 19, pp. 421–32.

self.[1] And though such communion does not remove all theological difficulties, it does, he believed, go some way towards it and it certainly delivers the gospel preacher from being impeded by them:

'We are often in the dark, and puzzled about difficulties, but do you know half the difficulties in the Bible spring from a cold state of mind: but when the heart gets right, the head seems to get right too, in great measure. I remember a person puzzling himself fearfully with the passage in Scripture about Jesus weeping over Jerusalem. He went and looked at Dr Gill about it, he went to Thomas Scott about it, and he went to Matthew Henry about it; and these good divines all puzzled him as much as they could, but they did not seem to clear up the matter. The good man could not understand how Jesus Christ could say as he did, "How oft would I have gathered thee, but thou wouldest not!" One day he received more grace, and got a love for souls, and then the old skin of narrow mindedness which had been large enough for him once began to crack and break, and he went to the passage then, and said, "I can understand it now; I do not know how it is consistent with such and such doctrine, but it is very consistent with what I feel in my heart." And I feel just the same. I used to be puzzled by that passage where Paul says that he could wish himself accursed from God for his brethren's sake. Why, I have often felt the same, and now understand how a man can say in the exuberance of love to others, that he would

[1] On this see *MTP*, vol. 35, p. 344. ('Perhaps the most difficult thing in soul winning is to get ourselves into a fit state ... the careless will be unmoved by any man who is unmoved himself. Tears storm a passage for warning'.) *The Soul Winner* (London, 1895), pp. 46-7. But the subject is dealt with in innumerable places by Spurgeon.

be willing to perish himself if he could save them. Of course it never could be done, but such is the extravagance of a holy love for souls that it breaks through reason, and knows no bounds.'[1]

It was Spurgeon's own persuasion of the love of Christ for the souls of men that lies at the heart of his weekly evangelistic preaching in London for thirty-seven years. He had no hesitation in concluding sermons with such words as, 'Cast yourself upon the Saviour's love, and you shall go down to your house justified'.[2] Or again: 'With hands loaded with love he stands outside the door of your heart. Is not this good reason for opening the door and letting the heavenly stranger in, when he can bless you with such a vast extent of benediction?'[3] Sometimes he made direct reference to his own experience, as in the sermon 'Compel Them To Come In', which was possibly more used in the conversion of people than any other which he ever preached. In that sermon he demanded obedience to the gospel, 'Sinner, in God's name I *command* you to repent and believe'. But after pressing this home he went on to entreat:

'Do you turn away and say you will not be commanded? Then again will I change my note ... I exhort you to flee to Christ. O my brother, dost thou know what a loving Christ he is? Let me tell thee from my own soul what I know of him ... I thought that Christ was cruel and unkind. O I can never forgive myself that I should have thought so ill of

---

[1] *MTP*, vol. 12, pp. 586–7. In another powerful reference to Christ weeping over Jerusalem, Spurgeon applies it to the 'brother who holds very high doctrines in his head, but has not much sympathy in his heart' (*MTP*, vol. 8, p. 347).

[2] *MTP*, vol. 33, p. 120.          [3] *MTP*, vol. 14, p. 200.

him. But what a loving reception did I have when I went to him. I thought he would smite me, but his hand was not clenched in anger but opened wide in mercy ... his eyes were full of tears. He fell on my neck and kissed me ... I entreat you to stop and consider. Do you know what it is you are rejecting this morning? You are rejecting Christ, your only Saviour ... I should be worse than a fiend if I did not now, with all love and kindness, and earnestness, beseech you to "lay hold on eternal life", "to labour not for the meat that perisheth, but for the meat that endureth unto everlasting life."

'Some Hyper-Calvinist would tell me I am wrong in so doing. I cannot help it. I must do it. As I must stand before my Judge at last, I feel that I should not make full proof of my ministry unless I entreat with many tears that ye would be saved, that ye would look to Jesus Christ and receive his glorious salvation.'[1]

Spurgeon is here saying no more than John Duncan, another Calvinist, said in the words: 'The gospel does not say, "There is a Saviour, if you wish to be saved;" but, "Sir, you have no right to go to hell – you can't go there without trampling on the Son of God." '[2]

\* \* \*

From what has been said above on the universal love of God, Hyper-Calvinists deduced that Spurgeon did not

---

[1] *NPSP*, vol. 5, pp. 20–2. In the Preface to this volume he comments: 'The sermon entitled "Compel them to come in" has been so signally owned of God, that scarcely a week occurs without some cases of its usefulness coming to light. The violent, rigid school of Calvinists will, of course, abhor the sermon.'

[2] *In the Pulpit and at the Communion Table*, p. 63.

believe in a special electing love which secures the salvation of all those for whom Christ died. Sometimes Christians of Arminian persuasion, with a superficial knowledge of Spurgeon, have reached the same conclusion on Spurgeon's position. But this is the same mistake as can be made in reading the Bible itself. *All* references to divine love in Scripture are not to be interpreted as universal (Arminianism), neither are they *all* to be made particular (Hyper-Calvinism). There is a differentiation observable in Scripture. In speaking to *Christians* Spurgeon would often make the difference clear: 'Beloved, the benevolent love of Jesus is more extended than the lines of his electing love ... That [i.e. the love revealed in Matthew 23:37] is not the love which beams resplendently upon his chosen, but it is true love for all that.'[1] God's special love 'is not love for all men ... There is an electing, discriminating, distinguishing love, which is settled upon a chosen people ... and it is this love which is the true resting place for the saint.'[2]

Arminianism, by making universal benevolence the *only* love revealed in Scripture, denies the sovereignty of grace and leads men to suppose that God had to make salvation equally available to all. Hyper-Calvinism, on the other hand, denies, in the words of John Murray, 'that there is a love of God that goes forth to lost men and is manifested in the manifold blessings which all men without distinction enjoy, a love in which non-elect persons are embraced, and a love that comes to its highest expression in the entreaties, overtures and demands of gospel proclamation.'[3]

[1] *MTP*, vol. 12, p. 475.
[2] *MTP*, vol. 19, p. 551. 'There is some consolation in universal benevolence, but here we must go deeper.'
[3] 'The Atonement and the Free Offer of the Gospel' in the *Banner of Truth* (London, 1968), July–August, p. 29.

While holding firmly to these important theological distinctions, Spurgeon did not believe that they were ones which had necessarily to be introduced in presenting the gospel to the unconverted and he warned against the kind of preaching which appears more concerned to safeguard orthodoxy than to save the lost. 'Many good people think they ought to guard the gospel ... When we protect it with provisos, and guard it with exceptions, and qualify it with observations, it is like David in Saul's armour.'[1]

He refused to explain how men could be held accountable for not trusting in a Saviour in whom they were never chosen, on the grounds that Scripture itself offers no explanation. It was enough for him that there is a salvation to be preached with love to all and that he call all to come to Christ and to say, 'If he died for all those who trust him, I will trust him; if he has offered so great a sacrifice upon the tree for guilty men, I will rely upon that sacrifice and make it the basis of my hope.'[2]

\*   \*   \*

These, then, are the four main points at which Spurgeon disagreed with Hyper-Calvinism – its restriction of gospel invitations, its failure to treat the word and promises of God as sufficient warrant for faith, its minimising of the place of human responsibility, and its denial of any love in God except love to the elect.

---

[1] *MTP,* vol. 32, p. 50.

[2] *MTP,* vol. 19, p. 280. He did not complain of 'Arminian friends' who preached 'very sweetly' on the breadth of Christ's love 'for they are the means of bringing in many converts who might not be brought in if it were not for their broad preaching', but he wished they understood more of its *length* (*MTP,* vol. 12, p. 478).

# 6

## The Aftermath

As with all controversies, this dispute seems to have polarised the parties in disagreement. Some Particular Baptists sided with Spurgeon and entered a new alignment. It is noticeable, for instance, that George Wyard of Deptford took part in the opening of the Metropolitan Tabernacle in 1861.[1] In 1871, however, when the Metropolitan Association of Strict Baptist Churches was formed, men who took Spurgeon's position on gospel preaching were excluded by article seven of the doctrinal basis which stated that 'saving faith is not a legal duty'. Meanwhile the ministers supporting the *Earthen Vessel* and the *Gospel Standard* had been split by a different controversy relating to the person of Christ. The issue was not his deity but rather the relationship between his person and his office as mediator. (Spurgeon deplored this controversy and the spectacle of Christians 'denouncing each other heartily'.)[2] Thereafter the Hyper-Calvinist Baptists were split between *Standard* men and *Vessel* men. Spurgeon regretted the spiritual decline which seemed to mark most of their

[1] In reviewing a book by Wyard, Spurgeon wrote of him, as one 'who is as sound in doctrine as he is loving in spirit' (*ST*, 1871, p. 235).

[2] *MTP*, vol. 9, p. 234. His statement shows that he saw both magazines.

churches. In 1876 he refers to the 'decadence' of Gill's 'rigid system'.[1] In an article on 'The Present Position of Calvinism in England' he wrote of 'Exaggerated Calvinism' being 'on the wane'. 'Its leading ministers have fallen of late like leaves in autumn, and their successors are not forthcoming ... We believe that these brethren, whatever their failings may have been, have done good service in keeping much precious truth stirring among the churches; and we should therefore rejoice to see them renew their youth, with more loving hearts and candid minds. They have been far too much despised and slighted. They ought not to be driven into isolation, but their alliance should be sought by their other Baptist brethren, and Christian intercourse would lead to mutual advantage.'[2]

But while a minority section of the Strict and Particular Baptist churches were becoming further entrenched and confirmed in Hyper-Calvinism, a larger number were moving away from Calvinism altogether and it was this fact which explained the doctrinal indifference which had come to prevail in the Baptist Union which Spurgeon left in 1888. In an article by R. Shindler in the *Sword and the Trowel,* published in 1889, it was said: 'At the present date, a very large number of so-called Particular Baptist churches and ministers have very little practical acquaintance with the 1689 Confession ... they ... have very little, if any, sympathy with the Confessions as a whole, and deny *in toto* some of its articles, such as relate to Election, Particular Redemption, Final Perseverance,

[1] *Commenting and Commentaries* (repr. Banner of Truth, 1969), p. 8.
[2] *ST,* 1874, pp. 49–53.

and the Punishment of the finally impenitent'.[1] At that date the General Baptists (Arminian) had not formally joined the Baptist Union but, as Shindler pointed out, there was obviously nothing to stop them. It would be well, he went on, 'for all who disown the Confession of 1689 to class themselves with the Generals; and all who own that Confession to bear the appellation of Particulars.'

The call for the 1689 Confession as a rallying point for true Calvinists could not, however, be heeded by the Hyper-Calvinists who, instead of returning to seventeenth-century standards, were now forming new articles of their own in a sincere but misguided effort to stop the drift to Arminianism.[2] They failed to see that a more balanced, biblical position would prove the best defence and were fearful of such an alliance as Spurgeon looked for. Thus in 1878 the *Gospel Standard* men added to their articles of faith. These articles already contained the assertions: 'We deny duty-faith and duty-repentance', and, 'We deny ... that the gospel is to be offered indiscriminately to all', but two new articles now asserted:

'We believe that it would be unsafe, from the brief records we have of the way in which the apostles, under the immediate direction of the Lord, addressed their hearers in certain special cases and circumstances, to derive universal and absolute rules for the ministerial addresses of the present day under widely different circumstances ... For ministers of the present day to address unconverted

---

[1] *ST,* 1899, p. 601. The author had also written the crucial 'Down-Grade' articles in 1887.

[2] Criticism of the Puritans and aspects of their creeds by such writers as Philpot had done its work (e.g. *Gospel Standard,* 1858, p. 288; 1861, p. 58).

persons, or indiscriminately all in a mixed congregation, calling upon them to savingly repent, believe, and receive Christ, or perform any other acts dependent upon the new creative power of the Holy Ghost, is, on the one hand, to imply creature power, and, on the other, to deny the doctrine of special redemption.'[1]

The tone of references to Spurgeon in the *Gospel Standard* magazine was commonly a great deal more hostile than in the *Earthen Vessel*. Indeed, the latter, in 1866, included a surprising admission from none other than James Wells himself. In the course of a letter to Banks for publication in the *Vessel*, in which he reviewed the situation as he saw it, Wells wrote:

'I admire the *decision* of the *Standard* party; but I cannot approve the spirit in which that decision is maintained. A spirit which has made and is making sad havoc in the churches, setting brother against brother, and despising every minister who does not choose to sacrifice to their net … When will Joseph's brethren cease to fall out by the way, error be checked, ungodliness rolled back, the chariot of salvation go majestically on; *little opinions* and little differences be treated as such, and zeal for the practical and saving truths of the gospel eat up ministers and Christians alike? Not in this generation, I fear. Differ as I do from Mr Spurgeon, yet he has shewn an independence of judgment, a magnanimity of soul, a nobleness of mind, and a range of benevolent feeling, enough to shame the hypers to a man.'[2]

---

[1] *What Gospel Standard Baptists Believe: a Commentary on the Gospel Standard Articles of Faith*, J. H. Gosden (repr. Chippenham: Gospel Standard Societies, 1993), p. 150.

[2] *Earthen Vessel*, 1866, p. 317.

In Wells' last illness, Spurgeon wrote him a private letter of sympathy, expressing the hope that he would 'play the man' in his affliction as he had long done in the pulpit.[1] The old pastor of Surrey Tabernacle thanked him in print for 'his kind and excellent letter' and spoke much of his failure as 'a poor weak mortal'. A reviewer in the *Gospel Standard* commented: 'A happy day would it be to see Mr Spurgeon brought to a like spot in his soul feelings. "Play the man," indeed ... Once let him, or other Duty-faith men be brought here, and away will go their duty-faith ... they will prove that though such flesh-pleasing doctrines may do while in the vigour of health, they will not do on a dying bed.'[2]

Banks would never have dreamed of writing in such a vein as this reviewer. In 1871 he referred to Spurgeon 'planting Open Communion churches, and a duty-faith ministry, all over this Island, and in the Colonies as far as is possible'; but he immediately added, 'unkindly or re-proachfully of Mr Spurgeon, we would never write or speak one word; having in his earlier years one most holy season of fellowship with him at the throne of God's mercy seat.'[3]

Many years later in 1886 Spurgeon included a column of typically generous words on Banks in the *Sword and the Trowel:*

'Mr Charles Waters Banks has passed away, after completing four-score years. He had a large heart, which

[1] *Letters of Charles Haddon Spurgeon,* pp. 73–4.

[2] *Gospel Standard,* 1874, p. 410, reviewing Wells' last publication, *Achor's Gloomy Vale. A Series of Letters addressed to the Church and Congregation.*

[3] *Earthen Vessel,* 1871, p. 11.

made him thoughtful of the poor, and tolerant of those who differed from him. In the dim past of thirty years and more, when certain ultra-calvinistic brethren were criticising us very severely, he expressed his friendliness for us as well as he could, for his position was a difficult one. He loved the doctrines of grace, but he did not like to smear them over with wormwood, as some of his comrades thought it wise to do. The old-fashioned high Calvinists are passing away, and we are among those who miss them. They may not have been all that we could have desired them to be, but they were good men and true, and believed firmly what the Lord had taught them. They were so resolved to hold what they did know that they were not in a hurry to learn more, and consequently missed some of the truths which make up the complete evangelical circle. Still, it was a great point about them that they were faithful to light received.

'Their places are not occupied by better men. The dominant, or at least the prominent faction, nowadays, believes in nothing but its own cleverness; and its pretended liberality derides all positive and fixed belief. We would sooner have the narrowness of those who have gone than the emptiness of those who ridicule them. Charles Waters Banks spent his life in preaching and writing for the cause he loved. In his old age he was as indefatigably industrious as in his youth; and he was always thoroughly unselfish, ready to help others, even when he might rather have asked help for himself.'[1]

---

[1] *ST,* 1886, p. 246. For Spurgeon on J. C. Philpot, long-time editor of the *Gospel Standard*, see *ST,* 1870, p. 332: 'We have read Mr Philpot's sermons with much profit; he was incomparable on his one theme, and now that he has gone to his reward, we will not write a

A review of the biography of another Strict Baptist pastor of Hyper-Calvinist persuasion, John Hazelton, in 1889, was written in the same generous vein, even though W. J. Styles, the biographer, had been a student at Spurgeon's College before changing his views. In the course of his review of *John Hazelton: a Memoir,* Spurgeon wrote:

'To us this biography has furnished special enjoyment, for Mr Hazelton came from our own town of Colchester, and became a member of that same Baptist church with which we often worshipped. Many of the names mentioned awaken happy memories in our heart. Mr Hazelton was led to embrace what we should have called *hyper-Calvinism,* if we had not seen from these pages that the word is distasteful ... Mr Hazelton faithfully adhered to those views which were advocated by Dr Gill; but he held them with courtesy and peacefulness ... Those who love the doctrines of sovereign grace will be refreshed by the allusions here made to the good men, now departed, who stood firm in their day. Many of these we knew and esteemed. Those religionists who will not see the special beauty of the Strict Particular Baptist, might do themselves a service and a pleasure if they were to read this memoir, to see the nature of "the sect which is everywhere spoken

---

word of that friendly criticism which were he living we might feel called upon to utter.' See also his remarks on the 'Standard Connection' in his magazine for 1872, p. 144. For a review of an Anglican Hyper-Calvinist ('a Particular Baptist who had lost his way and stumbled into a rectory') see his words on *Memorials of the Rev. Charles Rolfe, ST,* 1879, p. 491: 'The type is too narrow, but it is built for strength, and strength is needed now.'

against" … The points of difference between us and friends like brethren Hazelton and Styles are not unimportant; but we have far more points in common. We wish prosperity to the churches holding strong doctrine: may they be multiplied."[1]

\* \* \*

Before the end of the last century all forms of Calvinistic belief were being cast aside, and Spurgeon rightly predicted that fifty years might have to pass before there was a restoration of truth. But in the providence of God when that restoration began in the 1950s it was Spurgeon's position which exercised the major influence. Baptist magazines which were Calvinistic yet opposed to Hyper-Calvinism reappeared. The first of these was the *Free Grace Record,* edited by John C. Doggett from 1954, followed later by *Reformation Today.* Erroll Hulse, the editor of the latter, has also expounded Spurgeon's position on the general invitations of the gospel, as distinct from 'altar calls', in *The Great Invitation* (Welwyn: Evangelical Press, 1986). Similarly the denial of 'duty-faith'

---

[1] *ST,* 1889, p. 37. This spirit was not reciprocated by Hazelton's son, John E. Hazelton in his book *'Hold Fast!'* (London: Robert Banks, 1909), which contained sketches of English Calvinistic leaders but excluded Spurgeon. This book illustrates the degree of historical ignorance prevalent among such writers, for immediately after condemning free-offer preaching, Hazelton commends 'the truths formulated at Dort' (pp. 14–16) where the very teaching he attacks was upheld! But the *Autobiography of a Soldier in India,* written from a harsh and narrow Hyper-Calvinistic viewpoint, received different treatment from Spurgeon (*ST,* 1889, p. 239).

disappeared from several revised statements of belief[1] among the Calvinistic Baptists. It is possible that Spurgeon's thinking had come to have a greater effect upon the minds of younger ministers than had been the case in the previous century.[2]

It is also noteworthy that the return to Spurgeon's position coincided with a return to the Particular Baptist founding fathers. As Robert Oliver writes:

'A fresh examination of the seventeenth century confessions came as a part of a widespread movement of evangelical Christians of all denominations who were looking again at Reformed and Puritan theology. Many discerned in the writings of earlier theologians a depth and also a breadth which had been absent from much of the thought of more recent years. For Baptists a recovery of the seventeenth century confessions of faith resulted in a reassessment of much nineteenth century theologising.'[3]

In 1921 William Robertson Nicoll, editor of the *British Weekly*, wrote to a friend, 'I am sorry to see so many of the good old Calvinistic Baptist chapels vanishing away.'[4] In the subsequent halting of that decline we have a wonderful illustration of how God may use a man's testimony long

---

[1] See the article by Kenneth Dix, 'Particular Baptists and Strict Baptists', published by the Strict Baptist Historical Society, 1976.

[2] An example of this can be seen in *The Sound of His Name, Autobiography of Bernard J. Honeysett* (Banner of Truth, 1995).

[3] 'The Significance of Strict Baptist Attitudes towards Duty Faith in the Nineteenth Century', Robert W. Oliver, Strict Baptist Historical Society Bulletin, No. 20, 1993, pp. 24–5.

[4] *William Robertson Nicoll, Life and Letters*, T. H. Darlow (London: Hodder and Stoughton, 1925), p. 453.

after his death. Commenting once on the text, 'Cast thy bread upon the waters: for thou shalt find it after many days' (*Eccles.* 11:1), Spurgeon once said: 'We must not expect to see an immediate reward for all the good we do … His good word which we have spoken shall live. Perhaps not just yet, but some day we shall reap what we have sown.'[1]

Some, at least, of Spurgeon's contemporaries foresaw the truth of these words. William Williams, writing in 1895, recalled hearing his friend once say, 'I beseech you to live not only for this age, but for the next also', and he was sure Spurgeon had done this:

'His work is as imperishable as the truth of God. His memory shall not fade like a vanishing star, nor his works be forgotten like a dying echo. He will shine on, never ceasing to brighten human lives by the truth he preached, the work he accomplished, and the stainless life he lived.'[2]

---

[1] *The Cheque Book of the Bank of Faith*, entry for June 1.

[2] Williams, *Personal Reminiscences,* pp. 85–6.

# 7

## *Lessons from the Conflict*

1. Genuine evangelical Christianity is never of an exclusive spirit. Any view of the truth which undermines catholicity has gone astray from Scripture. This was the point which played a considerable part in Spurgeon's inability to join with the Strict Baptists. He could speak of them as 'about the best people in the world,'[1] but the practice of many of their churches in restricting the Lord's table to Baptists grieved him. Christians may be divided over their beliefs concerning the outward sign; they are not divided in the spiritual reality symbolised: 'I always say to Strict Baptist brethren who think it a dreadful thing for baptized believers to commune with the unbaptized: "But you cannot help it; if you are the people of God you must commune with all saints, baptized or not. You may deny them the outward and visible sign, but you cannot keep them from the inward spiritual grace." If a man be a child of God, I do not care what I may think about him – if he be a child of God I *do* commune with him and I must.'[2]

But he saw this professed separation of Strict Communion Baptists from the rest of the visible church was

[1] *NPSP*, vol. 4, p. 23.

[2] *MTP*, vol. 7, p. 83. There are many similar words elsewhere. See his anecdote on the subject, *MTP*, vol. 9, p. 152–3.

frequently made the more serious by the tenets of Hyper-Calvinism. Its teachers, from Huntington onwards, had commonly made faith in election a part of saving faith and thus either denied the Christianity of all professed Christians who did not so believe, or at least, treated such profession with much suspicion.[1] In so doing they had spread the idea that Calvinism is necessarily exclusive, that there is something inherent in its tenets which leads men to separate from others. Spurgeon deplored the way that the abuse of the doctrine of election had thus been used to foster division:

'We give our hand to every man that loves the Lord Jesus Christ, be he what he may or who he may. The doctrine of election, like the great act of election itself, is intended to divide, not between Israel and Israel, but between Israel and the Egyptians, – not between saint and saint, but between saints and the children of the world. A

---

[1] 'They are always flavoured with the thought of shutting others out. They are told that in such-and-such a Church there has been a large increase. Well, they hope they are genuine; by which they mean that they do not believe they are. A young believer begins to tell them something of his joys. Well, they don't like to be too fast in pronouncing an opinion; by which they mean that they would not like one more to get in than should, and they are half afraid that perhaps some may overstep the bounds of election and get saved who should not be' (*MTP*, vol. 8, p. 58). 'A mouse had lived in a box all its life, and one day crawled up to the edge of it, and looked round on what he could see. Now the box only stood in the lumber room, but the mouse was surprised at its vastness, and exclaimed, "How big the world is!" If some bigots would get out of their box, and only look a little way round them, they would find the realm of grace to be far wider than they dream' (*MTP*, vol. 17, p. 449). 'There will be more in heaven than we expect to see there by a long way' (*MTP*, vol. 12, p. 477).

man may be evidently of God's chosen family, and yet though elected, may not believe in the doctrine of election. I hold there are many savingly called, who do not believe in effectual calling, and that there are a great many who persevere to the end, who do not believe the doctrine of final perseverance. We do hope that the hearts of many are a great deal better than their heads. We do not set their fallacies down to any wilful opposition to the truth as it is in Jesus, but simply to an error in their judgments, which we pray God to correct. We hope that if they think us mistaken too, they will reciprocate the same Christian courtesy; and when we meet around the cross, we hope that we shall ever feel that we are one in Christ Jesus.'[1]

Spurgeon, as we have already seen in his attitude to Wells, practised this same catholicity in his relations with Christians of Hyper-Calvinist views, but this did not prevent him from speaking very strongly about the tendency of those views to lead churches into a narrow and often powerless exclusiveness:

'I like an expansive religion ... But there are some people so selfish that, provided they go to heaven, it is enough – they are in the covenant. They are the dear people of God – generally dear at any price; a peculiar people – awfully peculiar they are, certainly: they are so different from other people, – there is no doubt about that. They say it is equal whether God ordains a man's life or death. They would sit still to hear men damned ... They seem to have no feeling for anyone but themselves. They

---

[1] *NPSP*, vol. 6, p. 303. Whitefield had earlier maintained the same attitude, *The Works of George Whitefield*, vol. 1 (London, 1771), p. 406.

have dried the heart out of them by some cunning sleight of hand.'[1]

This emphasis, though without the element of sarcasm in the last quotation, runs throughout his ministry. In a sermon of 1864 he said:

'True peace puts an end to all spiritual monopoly. I know there are some who think there is no grace beyond their own church ... not unlike those ancient wranglers in the land of Uz, they say, "We are the men and wisdom will die with *us*." Surely God's people never talk in that fashion, or if they do, they are then speaking the language of Ashdod and not the speech of the child of Israel, for the Israelite's tongue drops with love, and his speech is full of the anxious desire that others may be brought in. Look at our apostle Paul. You shall never find stronger pre-destinarianism than you read in the ninth chapter of Romans, and yet what does he say? His heart's desire and prayer to God for Israel is, that they might be saved.'[2]

Again, preaching in 1881 he said:

'You may have sound doctrine and yet do nothing unless you have Christ *in your spirit*. I have known all the doctrines of grace to be unmistakably preached, and yet there have been no conversions; for this reason, that they were not expected and scarcely desired. In former years many orthodox preachers thought it to be their sole duty to comfort and confirm the godly few who by dint of per-severance found out the holes and corners in which they prophesied. These brethren spoke of sinners as people

---

[1] *NPSP*, vol. 6, p. 450. His hardest words are, like these, directed at the Antinomian fatalists at the extreme of the Hyper-Calvinist spectrum.

[2] *MTP*, vol. 10, pp. 283–4.

whom God might possibly gather in if he thought fit to do so; but they did not care much whether he did so or not. As to weeping over sinners as Christ wept over Jerusalem; as to venturing to invite them to Christ as the Lord did when he stretched out his hands all the day long; as to lamenting with Jeremiah over a perishing people, they had no sympathy with such emotions, and feared they savoured of Arminianism. Both preacher and congregation were cased in a hard shell, and lived as if their own salvation was the sole design of their existence.[1]

2. This controversy brings out the danger which is created when biblical truths are constantly presented to the non-Christian in the wrong order. Spurgeon believed all the truths commonly called Calvinistic but he did not believe that all the truths commonly so designated had to be presented to sinners in order to their conversion. As noted, he wanted to see both divine sovereignty and human responsibility upheld but when it came to gospel preaching he believed that there needed to be a greater concentration upon responsibility. The tendency of Hyper-Calvinism was to make sinners want to understand theology before they could believe in Christ, as though

---

[1] *MTP*, vol. 27, p. 600. Spurgeon never set love over against the sound doctrine. He followed Scripture, however, in emphasising that doctrine alone is not enough. 'When love dies orthodox doctrine becomes a corpse, a powerless formalism. Adhesion to the truth sours into bigotry when the sweetness and light of love to Jesus depart ... Lose love, lose all' (*MTP*, vol. 32, pp. 580–1). Doctrinal discernment is not the only test to be applied to Christians: 'Some who have been great fools in doctrine have been very wise in love' (*MTP*, vol. 10, p. 142).

'they cannot be saved till they are thorough theologians.'[1] But the non-Christian can hear 'the soul and marrow of the gospel', that is, Christ as the Saviour, and see his responsibility to repent and believe, without understanding 'the doctrines commonly called Calvinistic'.[2] It is with his responsibility, says Spurgeon, that 'the sinner has the most to do', whereas God's predestinating grace is the subject with which 'the saint has most to do. Let him praise the free and sovereign grace of God, and bless his name'.[3]

In so thinking Spurgeon was surely siding with what the wisest preachers in the church had always taught. While Reformed Confessions may begin with statements on the doctrine of God and divine decrees, that is not where preachers and teachers need to begin in addressing men about salvation. In the apostolic preaching to the lost, recorded in the book of Acts, nothing is said of the doctrine of election, while in the Epistles 'it is scarcely ever omitted'.[4] In accordance with this approach, Calvin, in the later editions of his *Institutes,* moved his treatment of election to *follow* teaching on justification. He recognised that Scripture generally introduces the doctrine of election

[1] *NPSP,* vol. 4, p. 439.

[2] *MTP,* vol. 13, p. 706. 'If any man shall say that the preaching of these [doctrines] is the whole of the preaching of the gospel, I am at issue with him ... while the doctrines of election, final perseverance, and so on, go to make up a complete ministry, and are invaluable in their place, yet the soul and marrow of the gospel is not there, but is found in the great fact that "God was manifest in the flesh, justified in the Spirit," and so on. Preach Christ, young man, if you want to win souls. Preach all the doctrines, too, for the building up of believers.'

[3] *NPSP,* vol. 4, p. 343.

[4] Crawford, *Mysteries of Christianity*, p. 364.

to show *believers* the security and certainty of their salvation and to make clear who made them to differ. But when election is constantly introduced as a preliminary to hearing the gospel it inevitably comes to be seen as though it were designed to limit or obstruct the salvation of men and women. No one put this point better than John Bradford, the English reformer, whose words were often quoted by Whitefield, 'Let a man go to the grammar school of faith and repentance, before he goes to the university of election and predestination.'[1]

It ought not to be the business of the evangelist to teach God's decrees to the unconverted. It is certainly God's decree of salvation which is fulfilled in conversion but knowledge of that decree is no part of saving faith. As Crawford says, God's decrees are his fixed purposes and his 'secret designs for the regulation of his own procedure; *but they are not rules or laws prescribed for the guidance of others* ... The doctrine of election is not to be regarded as what an apostle calls the "milk that babes have need of," but as the "strong meat that belongs to them who are of full age." It ought not, therefore, to be *prefixed to the* calls of the Gospel, or placed in the fore-front of the calls and invitations which are therein addressed without restriction to all sinners. When so placed, it is apt to perplex and disquiet humble souls ... No man can be of the number of the elect if he utterly neglects the appointed means of salvation; and no man can be of the number of the non-elect if he truly repents and unfeignedly believes the

[1] *George Whitefield's Journals* (Banner of Truth, 1960), p. 491. Whitefield added, 'A bare head-knowledge of sound words availeth nothing.'

Gospel. The salvation of a sinner *is actually brought to pass,* according to the plainest declarations of Holy Scripture, *in the way of faith and repentance, and no otherwise.*[1]

3. This controversy directs us to our need for profound humility before God. It reminds us forcefully of questions about which we can only say, 'Behold, God is great, and we know him not' (*Job* 36:26), and, 'O the depth of the riches both of the wisdom and knowledge of God! how unsearchable are his judgments, and his ways past finding out!' (*Rom.* 11:33). We do not know why God has purposed to save some and not others, nor why, given his desire for the good of all, many are left in their sin. We cannot say why his love to all men is not the same as his love to the elect. We do not know how God works in us 'to will and to do' and yet leaves us wholly responsible for our own actions, nor how invitations to all to believe on Christ for salvation are to be harmonised with electing grace. As Crawford said, various attempts have been made to solve such mysteries, 'but, it must be owned, they have been signally unsuccessful.' He concludes: 'We do well to be exceedingly diffident in our judgments respecting matters so unsearchable as the secret purposes of God.'[2]

It is to be feared that sharp contentions between Christians on these issues have too often arisen from a wrong confidence in our powers of reasoning and our assumed ability to draw logical inferences. It is arguable that in the eclipse of Calvinistic beliefs at the beginning of the eighteenth century, at a time when 'reason' was being made the

---

[1] *Mysteries of Christianity,* pp. 317, 363, 338.
[2] *Mysteries of Christianity,* pp. 273, 357.

test of all religious belief, the would-be defenders of orthodoxy who became Hyper-Calvinistic fell into the very
mistake which they were seeking to correct. As J. I. Packer
writes, 'In an increasingly rationalistic age, the reaction
itself was rationalistic, within the Reformed super-
naturalistic frame.'[1] Joseph Hussey, the standard bearer of
the movement, certainly gave justification for that charge.
The contentious spirit in which he advocated his views
was a discredit to the truth. John Newton was not the
only Calvinist to complain that in Hussey's writings, 'I
frequently found more bones than meat, and seasoned with
much of an angry and self-important spirit.'[2]

Spurgeon, like all the children of men, had to learn
humility, and he was not always entirely blameless in this
regard in his early years, but it was given to him to see how
a system which sought to attribute all to the grace of God
had itself too much confidence in the powers of reason. His
mature judgment on that point, given below, constitutes
a statement of great value.[3] Probably as a young man
Spurgeon was, at times, over-concerned to assert his
agreement with Calvin but in his deepening humility
before God, and his refusal to trust in human reason, he

---

[1] In Toon, *Hyper-Calvinism,* p. 7. See also p. 147. A contributor to
the Eclectic Society of Anglican evangelicals said in 1801: 'Fuller's
*Gospel Worthy of All Acceptation*, is a work of great use. Hussey was the
first who started this question. The Old Calvinists never thought of it.'
*The Thought of the Evangelical Leaders,* ed. J. H. Pratt (1856; repr.
Banner of Truth, 1978).

[2] Letter 1 of 'Nine letters to the Rev. Mr R.' [i.e. John Ryland, Jr.) in
*Cardiphonia; or, The Utterance of the Heart* (London: Nelson, 1857),
p. 362.

[3] See below pp. 149-54.

truly followed in the spirit of that leader and of all true teachers in the church of God. It was Calvin, shortly before his death, who, on the words, 'Have I any pleasure at all that the wicked should die? saith the Lord God: and not that he should return from his ways, and live?' (*Ezek.* 18:23) said this: 'If anyone again objects – this is making God act with duplicity, the answer is ready, that God always wishes the same thing, though by different ways, and in a manner inscrutable to us. Although, therefore, God's will is simple, yet great variety is involved in it, as far as our senses are concerned. Besides, it is not surprising that our eyes should be blinded by intense light, so that we cannot judge how God wishes all to be saved, and yet has devoted all the reprobate to eternal destruction, and wishes them to perish. While we look now through a glass darkly, we should be content with the measure of our own intelligence (*1 Cor.* 13:12).'[1]

---

[1] *Commentaries on the Prophet Ezekiel,* vol. 2 (Edinburgh, 1850), pp. 247–8. A friend, James Greenbury, pointed me to an article very relevant to these pages. C. P. Venema writing on 'Heinrich Bullinger's Correspondence on Calvin's Doctrine of Predestination, 1551–1553,' says that while Bullinger rejected Melanchthon's synergism, he taught: (1) that the apostles 'understood God to desire well of all men,' wanting all to be saved and to come to the knowledge of the truth; (2) that 'those who perish do not perish by virtue of being compelled by a fatal necessity, but because they willingly reject the grace of God'; (3) that those who are saved are saved by 'the mere grace of God,' understanding faith to be his gift. (*The Sixteenth Century Journal XVII,* 1986), pp. 439–42. After his fiftieth birthday, Spurgeon once said: 'In theology I stand where I did when I began preaching, and I stand almost alone … I stand almost exactly where Calvin stood in his maturer years; – not where he stood in his *Institutes*, which he wrote when quite a young man, but in his later works; that position is taken

4.   The final conclusion has to be that when Calvinism ceases to be evangelistic, when it becomes more concerned with theory than with the salvation of men and women, when acceptance of doctrines seems to become more important than acceptance of Christ, then it is a system going to seed and it will invariably lose its attractive power. As we have seen, in his early ministry Spurgeon was opposed by those who believed that the Hyper-Calvinism of such eighteenth-century Baptists as John Gill represented the purest Christianity under heaven. That interpretation of history he knew to be wrong, not simply because it fell short of Scripture, but because its effect was to reduce endeavours for the conversion of sinners. 'During the pastorate of my venerated predecessor, Dr Gill, this Church, instead of increasing, gradually decreased ... But mark this, from the day when Fuller, Carey, Sutcliffe, and others, met together to send out missionaries to India the sun began to dawn of a gracious revival which is not over yet.'[1]

In this connection it is noteworthy that just as renewed understanding of the free offer of the gospel led to the age of overseas missions in England so it did also – by different means – in Scotland. As James Walker writes, Boston and the Marrow men 'entered fully into the missionary spirit of

---

by few' (*C. H. Spurgeon: The Full Harvest,* p. 393). Spurgeon did not appear to appreciate that Calvin's *Institutes* was revised more than once. The truth is probably that Calvin could have said with Spurgeon, 'I would sooner a hundred times over be inconsistent with myself than be inconsistent with the word of God.'

[1] *MTP,* vol. 11, p. 428. See *ST,* 1883, pp. 72–5; and *One Heart and One Soul: John Sutcliff of Olney, his friends and his times,* Michael A. G. Haykin (Darlington: Evangelical Press, 1994).

the Bible' and 'were able to see that Calvinistic doctrine is not inconsistent with world-conquering aspirations and efforts.'[1] Robert Moffat, Scots pioneer missionary in South Africa, was one of the outstanding results of this rediscovery. A Calvinist who made the Shorter Catechism of the Westminster Assembly one of the first publications of the infant mission press at Kuruman, Moffat had no hesitation in writing as follows in 1834:

'I see nothing in the world worth looking after if it has not a direct reference to the glory and extension of the Redeemer's kingdom; and were we always able to have a lively view of the myriads who are descending to the horrible pit, our zeal would be proportionate. Much depends on us who have received the ministry of reconciliation, assured that God our Saviour willeth the salvation of all.'[2]

To say this is not to deny that there have been preachers of Hyper-Calvinistic views whose preaching has been used in the conversion of many. Spurgeon was thankful for such men as John Warburton and John Kershaw, men whose Christ-centredness often enabled them to rise above their system.[3] But in the hands of the general run of men who regarded Hyper-Calvinism as scriptural he believed the tendency of the preaching was inevitably injurious. By

[1] James Walker, *The Theology and Theologians of Scotland* (Edinburgh, 1872), p. 60.

[2] John S. Moffat, *The Lives of Robert and Mary Moffat* (London: T. Fisher Unwin, n.d.), p. 124. On the text to which Moffat makes allusion (*1 Tim.* 2:4) see below, p. 149.

[3] See *Memorials of John Warburton*, ed. G. Hemington (London: F. Kirby, 1892), and *John Kershaw, 1792–1870, Autobiography* (repr. Sheffield: Gospel Tidings Publications, 1968).

distorting and exaggerating truth the system misrepresented vital doctrines and made them offensive instead of appealing to the wider Christian world. He was convinced that the truths called Calvinistic would never be more widely received among the churches if the impression was allowed to prevail that these truths inhibited earnest evangelism, as they commonly did where Hyper-Calvinism became the accepted tradition. 'I have seen,' he says, 'to my inexpressible grief, the doctrines of grace made a huge stone to be rolled at the mouth of the sepulchre of a dead Christ.'[1]

Hyper-Calvinism still exists today but what is needed far more than a renewed controversy on the subject is living evidence that the doctrines of grace are harmonious with true evangelistic preaching. The ministries of such men as Whitefield, Spurgeon and, more recently, Lloyd-Jones, proved that more than a thousand books could ever do. Such preaching can only come from a baptism of new and deeper devotion to Christ. Much more than a change of opinion is needed. Spurgeon laboured all his ministry for purity of doctrine but his final word was always this:

'What is doctrine after all but the throne whereon Christ sitteth, and when the throne is vacant what is the throne to us? Doctrines are the shovel and tongs of the altar, while Christ is the sacrifice smoking thereon. Doctrines are Christ's garments; verily they smell of myrrh, and cassia, and aloes out of the ivory palaces, whereby they make us glad, but it is not the garments we care for as much as the person, the very person of our Lord Jesus Christ.'

---

[1] *MTP*, vol. 8, p. 339. There are many such warnings in his early sermons.

# PART THREE

*Illustrative Material*

'Men who are morbidly anxious to possess a self-consistent creed, a creed which will put together and form a square like a Chinese puzzle, – are very apt to narrow their souls. Fancying that all truth can be comprehended in half-a-dozen formulae, they reject as worthless every doctrinal statement which cannot be so comprehended. Those who will only believe what they can reconcile will necessarily disbelieve much of divine revelation. They are, without knowing it, following the lead of the rationalists. Those who receive by faith anything which they find in the Bible will receive two things, twenty things, ay, or twenty thousand things, though they cannot construct a theory which harmonises them all.'

SPURGEON on 'Faith'
*Sword and the Trowel,* 1872, p. 256.

# 8

## Two Illustrations –
## John Gill and William Huntington

Although Dr John Gill (1697–1771) died over sixty years before Spurgeon was born, the lives of the two men were connected at many points. In 1852, as a youth at Waterbeach, Spurgeon subscribed to Gill's Commentary which was then being republished in monthly instalments, and two years later he succeeded to the Southwark pastorate which Gill had once served. Thereafter he saw Gill's chair and his portrait constantly in his vestry, and his predecessor's pulpit eventually became the desk from which Spurgeon lectured in the Pastors' College. G. H. Pike wrote that in Spurgeon's 'early days, more particularly, he would refer at times to Dr Gill with great satisfaction.'[1] Our own reading of Spurgeon does not reveal any difference in his attitude to Gill in the course of his life. From the outset Spurgeon could speak with appreciation of the man while being critical of the Hyper-Calvinistic aspects of his theology. 'Dr Gill is not my rabbi', he would tell the congregation at New Park Street.[2] But with respect to Gill's writings as a whole Spurgeon always retained a degree of admiration and in 1879 we find him writing to his

[1] *Pike,* vol. 1, p. 123.
[2] *NPSP*, vol. 4, p. 344.

secretary, J. L. Keys, 'I want a good cheap copy of Gill's Commentary for my son Charles.'[1]

Gill was not the originator of what became the hallmark of Hyper-Calvinism, namely that preachers should not give general invitations to all to believe on Christ for salvation. This was first advanced by Joseph Hussey, a Congregationalist minister, who published his *God's Operations of Grace but No Offers of Grace* in 1707. Hussey's view was then promoted among the Calvinistic Baptists by John Skepp, a friend and encourager of the young John Gill. Called to the Baptist church then meeting at Horsleydown, Southwark, in 1719, at the age of twenty-two, Gill's position at the head of this important congregation, his erudition (subsequently acknowledged by Marischal College, Aberdeen, which conferred a doctorate in divinity in 1748), and his sanctity of life, all combined to give him an influence to spread the teaching which others were to embrace as orthodox Calvinism. Unlike many who were to follow him, Gill was aware of the change he was introducing for in 1729 he had led his congregation to adopt a new *Declaration of Faith and Practice* which omitted the usual Puritan references to Christ being offered in the gospel. With regard to the advance of Hussey's new teaching it is significant that there appear to have been no printings of the 1689 Baptist Confession for seventy years after 1720.

An article in the *Sword and the Trowel,* commenting on the change which came to the Particular Baptists in the eighteenth century, said:

'They did not give up Calvinism, or, in other words,

[1] *Letters of Charles Haddon Spurgeon*, p. 88.

renounce the Confession of 1689, but they overlaid it with an incrustation of something which approached Antinomianism, and ate out the life of the churches, and of the gospel as preached by many ministers. Divine sovereignty was maintained and taught, not only in exaggerated proportions, but to the practical exclusion of moral responsibility; the obligation of sinners to "repent and believe the gospel," was ignored, and even denied, and all gospel invitations and pleadings were restricted to those who were supposed to give evidence of a gracious state.'[1]

While Spurgeon did not write the above, it is clear that it represents his general view. His own words are: 'The system of theology with which many identify his [i.e., Gill's] name has chilled many churches to their very soul, for it has led them to omit the free invitations of the gospel, and to deny that it is the duty of sinners to believe in Jesus.'[2]

How far Gill was directly responsible for the condition of things which resulted has sometimes been argued. Certainly he did not hold the view, commonly identified with Antinomianism, which asserts that the moral law – as summarised in the ten commandments – is no rule of life for believers; nor did he believe in 'imputed sanctification,' and he was careful to repudiate any idea that God's judgment on sinners is a question of pure sovereignty. On such points some who succeeded him were to bring immense and unfair discredit upon all Hyper-Calvinists.

But Spurgeon would appear to be over-generous to Gill when he writes: 'Gill is the Coryphaeus of Hyper-Calvinism, but if his followers never went beyond their

[1] *ST*, 1889, p. 600.　　　　[2] *Autobiography*, 1897, vol. 1, p. 310.

master, they would not go very far astray.'[1] The keystone of
Hyper-Calvinistic thinking is clearly to be found in Gill
and especially in his two volumes, *The Cause of God and
Truth,* published to refute Arminianism. In these he argues
at length that men are not responsible for 'coming to him
[Christ], or believing in him to the saving of their souls,'
because they cannot so do 'without the special grace of
God'. Unregenerate men can only be called to an 'historic
faith', that is to say to an assent to the facts of the gospel. As
far as texts of Scripture were concerned, Gill believed, 'I
know of none that exhort and command all men, all the
individuals of the human race to repent, and believe
in Christ for salvation.'[2] His case is that men are only
obligated as far as the 'revelation' they receive. Men in
general are only given an 'external' revelation and with this
nothing more than an historical, not saving, faith can be
required of them. The elect, on the other hand, are given
an 'internal' revelation, making them 'sensible' of their lost
estate, acquainting them with Christ and thus leading them
'to venture on him, rely upon him, and believe in him.'[3]
The gospel makes no promises to 'dead men', only to
'sensible sinners'.[4]

In accordance with this, Gill claimed that all texts appearing to show a favourable desire on God's part towards
all the lost *do not* have any reference to their salvation.
Thus when God says, 'Why will ye die?' Gill believed
we are to understand: 'the death expostulated about, is
not eternal, but a temporal one, or what concerns their

---

[1] *Commenting and Commentaries*, p. 9.
[2] *The Cause of God and Truth* (new ed., London, 1814), vol. 2,
pp. 56–7.
[3] *Ibid.,* vol. 1, pp. 96–8.      [4] *Ibid.,* vol. 1, p. 63.

temporal affairs, and civil condition, and circumstances of life.'[1] Similarly, when Christ says, 'How often would I have gathered thy children …' it is to be understood not of gathering to salvation but only of a gathering to hear him preach and thus be brought to historical faith 'sufficient to preserve them from temporal ruin'. And the will of Christ to gather them 'is not to be understood of his divine will … but of his human will, or of his will as a man; which, though not contrary to the divine will, but subordinate to it, [is] yet not always the same with it, nor always fulfilled.'[2]

Spurgeon says that Gill 'must not be altogether held responsible' for the system of theology with which his name is identified yet he certainly cannot be exonerated from blame. After commending Gill for his learning, his labours and his sanctity of life, James Bennett in his *History of Dissenters* says that his writings contain more knowledge than wisdom and, 'It is above all to be lamented, that they have diffused a taste for extravagant Calvinism.'[3] Spurgeon pays tribute to Gill as a commentator, and notes that his Commentary contains 'expressions altogether out of accord with such a narrow scheme,'[4] but he has this serious reservation: 'Very seldom does he allow himself to be run away with by imagination, except now and then when he tries to open up a parable, and finds a meaning in every circumstance and minute detail; or when

[1] *Ibid.,* vol. 1, p. 77.

[2] *Ibid.,* vol. 1, pp. 87–8. See also vol. 2, p. 77. The same basic arguments are repeated through the two volumes.

[3] *The History of the Dissenters, from the Revolution to 1808,* J. Bennett (London, 1823), vol. 2, p. 642.

[4] *Autobiography,* 1897, vol. 1, p. 310.

he falls upon a text which is not congenial with his creed, and hacks and hews terribly to bring the word of God into a more systematic shape.'[1]

Joseph Ivimey (1773–1834), Baptist pastor and historian, draws attention to the inevitable effect which Gill's teaching had upon evangelistic preaching. After quoting from the conclusion of one of Gill's own sermons in which he addressed the unconverted, Ivimey noted:

'Here are no alarming appeals to the conscience, as when our Lord said, "Except ye repent ye shall perish". Here are no expostulations to urge them to serious consideration of the danger of sin, and unbelief, as when Paul declared, "For we must all appear before the judgment seat of Christ," etc. – "knowing, therefore, the terrors of the Lord we persuade men": – no "beseeching them in Christ's stead to be reconciled to God," from the sufficiency of the atonement and righteousness of Christ for the salvation and justification of all who believe in the name of Jesus:– no warnings of the awful doom of those who in addition to being ignorant of God, refused to "obey the gospel of Jesus Christ": – no exhortation to "flee from the wrath to come," by flying "for refuge to lay hold of the hope set before them": – no direction to pray for pardon, for grace, and mercy, through the mediation of Jesus; but they are merely told in reference to seeking their eternal salvation, "Attend the means of grace, and may the Lord call you by it in due time." Is this preaching Christ "the hope of glory" as Paul did?'[2]

---

[1] *Commenting and Commentaries*, p. 9.

[2] *History of the English Baptists*, Joseph Ivimey (London, 1823), vol. 3, pp. 460–1. See also his words on 'false Calvinism' (p. x) where he also draws attention to the Baptist departure from their 1689

Gill remained in his Southwark charge for over fifty years. By the time of his death in 1771 Hyper-Calvinism was waning. In large part this was due to the impact of the evangelical Calvinism of the Evangelical Revival on Nonconformist churches. As a recent writer has said, an age had come which was 'less and less impressed with rationality and more warmed by the flames of fervent revived religion. The High Calvinist position was lost less through argument than merely through the emergence of a new age with little interest in rationalism.'[1] With new evidence of the power of the Word of God breaking forth in the land there was less concern with the provision of a 'logical' defence of orthodoxy. James Upton was not the only Calvinistic Baptist who came to the conclusion that 'a fondness for controversy is not the road to extensive usefulness in winning souls to Christ.'[2]

It should also be said that not all Calvinistic Baptists had succumbed to Hyper-Calvinism. The Bristol Baptist Academy, for instance, appears to have produced a number of pastors who remained on the older foundation and among them was Gill's successor, John Rippon, who was

---

Confession. Thomas J. Nettles complains that Ivimey 'infers many things from silence rather than from direct statements in Gill's writings' but it is hard to see how Nettles' defence of Gill can be sustained (*By His Grace and for His Glory*, T. J. Nettles [Grand Rapids: Baker Book House, 1986], p. 86).

[1] *Continuity and Change: London Calvinistic Baptists and the Evangelical revival 1760–1820,* R. Philip Roberts (Wheaton, Illinois: Richard Owen Roberts, 1989), p. 166.

[2] *Ibid.*, p. 135, quoting from James Upton, *Letters on the Excellence and Influence of Evangelical Truth* (1819), p. 40.

called to Southwark in 1773. Rippon's call immediately led to controversy in the congregation and some forty members seceded in protest, it seems, that Gill's distinctive teaching on the points in controversy was no longer to be maintained. In his *Brief Memoir of the Life and Writings of the late John Gill,* the peace-loving Rippon is moderate in his references to Gill's Hyper-Calvinism but the main point of Gill's deviation from the seventeenth-century position is stated: 'Respecting the subject of what is called the Free Address to unconverted Sinners, certainly the two doctors took different sides. Dr Crisp was in practice of it, Dr Gill against it.'[1]

Towards the end of the eighteenth century the views of such men as Rippon came to coalesce with the convictions which Fuller and others had rediscovered in the Puritans and in Jonathan Edwards. 'By reading the works of Dr John Owen,' writes Bennett, Fuller found 'that there was one who harmonised with Bunyan in invitations to sinners, rather than with Gill and Brine, the oracles among his Baptist friends.'[2] It was in accord with this movement of thought that Rippon republished the 1689 Confession in 1790. Philip Roberts, who has detailed something of this

---

[1] *Brief Memoir of the Life and Writings of Gill,* J. Rippon, p. 71. Gill had reissued the works of Tobias Crisp, the Puritan, in 1755. Rippon points out (pp. 46–7) that Gill's treatment of John 5:40 in his Commentary was not in accord with what he had said elsewhere on human responsibility.

[2] *History of the Dissenters During the Last Thirty Years,* J. Bennett (London, 1839), p. 472. Bennett is noticeably pro-Puritan but anti-Hyper-Calvinist. He also observes that some English Calvinists were 'injudicious' in their use of Edwards as a champion (*History of the Dissenters From the Revolution,* vol. 2, p. 501).

transition, writes: 'In the course of the period 1760–1820 several Bristol Academy graduates filled London Calvinistic Baptist pulpits and represented perhaps the most vibrant force for change on behalf of evangelical Calvinism … By the turn of the century High Calvinism was, to all intents and purposes, a dead issue among Baptist Board-related churches.'[1]

It was precisely at this juncture that a new voice was heard in London. It might not be too much to claim that it was William Huntington (1745–1813) who preserved Hyper-Calvinism from near extinction. There were others at the time who adhered to Gill's position, including William Button, the pastor of the disaffected minority which broke away from Rippon's congregation in 1773. It was Button in 1785 who sought to refute Andrew Fuller. But Huntington was probably the first London preacher to show that one could be both a popular preacher and a vigorous upholder of Hyper-Calvinism. A self-educated man and, as he liked to remember, a one-time 'coalheaver', Huntington arrived in London in 1782. He was soon followed by such crowds that a new building, Providence Chapel, in Titchfield Street, was built for him. One of his biographers asserted, 'That Huntington was the greatest preacher of his day is indubitable,' though he thought it an exaggeration to say that as a teacher he was 'greater than any who had moved on the earth since the days of Paul.'[2]

---

[1] *Continuity and Change,* pp. 130–1. Roberts points to at least four London Baptist churches which moved out of the Hyper-Calvinist camp (p. 163).

[2] *The Life of William Huntington,* Thomas Wright (London: Farncombe, 1909), pp. 186, 138.

But though Huntington wrote about a hundred books of various sizes he can scarcely be described as a 'teacher' in any usual sense of the word. While there are fine devotional passages at times in his sermons and letters, no serious exposition of Scripture is offered. The main points of Hyper-Calvinism are all present and in the crudest form he consigned Arminians, John Wesley included, to hell. An unhappy bitterness between Christians of Arminian and Calvinistic persuasion had arisen temporarily in England in the 1770s[1] but Huntington did much to make it endemic among later Hyper-Calvinists.

To the already existing features of Hyper-Calvinism (notably the proneness to omit 'practical exhortation, invitations and warnings'),[2] Huntington added a denial that the ten commandments are a 'rule of life' for believers, a view hitherto associated only with Antinomians.[3] Not

[1] Speaking of this controversy, Bennett says: 'Both sides discovered, towards certain truths, feelings which did them honour; the one jealous for divine sovereignty and grace, with human dependence; the other for infinite justice and holiness, with the moral agency of man. But they seem to have reserved their religion for their friends, and to have thought that anything was lawful to an enemy. Forgetting that, from erring man, the errors, as well as sins, of his brother demand sorrow rather than anger; they let loose all the furies against their opponent's opinion.' *History of Dissenters From the Revolution*, vol. 2, p. 505.

[2] *The Celebrated Coalheaver; or, Reminiscences of the Rev William Huntington*, Ebenezer Hooper (London, 1871), p. 46.

[3] 'A rule of divine life the decalogue can never be' ('The Law Established by Faith in Christ', pp. 53–4 in *Huntington's Works* [London: Bensley], vol. 25). In attacking 'law' Huntington ignored the vital distinction which Rippon noted in writing of Gill: 'He everywhere maintains, with our best divines, that believers are delivered from it, totally delivered, having no just reason either to expect life from its

surprisingly Huntington was soon isolated from the main stream of evangelical Christianity – Calvinistic as well as Arminian – and he responded to the situation by denouncing all but a handful of his contemporaries. In an age of growing evangelical life and witness, with dramatic overflow into foreign missions and other evangelical agencies, Huntington could assert, 'making hypocrites is the work of this generation … I do not believe that there is one spiritual minister in London, nor do I know but three in the nation.'[1] This outlook went hand-in-hand with his disinterest in directing his hearers to the best Christian literature of the past. His disdain for books – 'dead men's brains' – was proverbial. He professed the intention to own the works of no commentators,[2] though those of Gill and one or two others were in his possession at his death.

---

promises, or to fear death from its threatenings. But that, as a RULE of *obedience*, it is of universal obligation, equally binding upon saints and sinners, and must remain so for ever, while God is God and man is man' (*Brief Memoir*, p. 100). Hooper says that by defending what was 'a novel and peculiar doctrine' Huntington 'unavoidably incurred the name of Antinomian'. After some strong criticism of Huntington, John Angell James wrote: 'What is Antinomianism? the gospel abstracted from law and resting upon a basis of sovereign mercy, instead of being founded upon the principles of moral government – a scheme intended to subvert law, while mercy is exercised towards its offenders. A true faith therefore, must be exercised as much towards all the duties of the law as towards all the blessings of the gospel' (*The Course of Faith, or the Practical Believer Delineated*, J. A. James [London, 1857], p. viii).

[1] *The Lamentations of Satan*, part 2, 1812, pp. 67-8; and *Celebrated Coalheaver*, Hooper, p. 44.

[2] *Select Works of Huntington* (London: Bennett, 1837), vol. 1, p. 168.

Huntington was a paedo-Baptist Independent but his enduring impact was chiefly among the Strict Baptists. Wells resembled him both in his theology and in the kind of dogmatic oratory which continued to draw crowds in London. There can be little doubt that the exclusiveness which Huntington's attitude engendered affected much of nineteenth-century Hyper-Calvinism and it was no accident that his name was to be most highly revered among the Gospel Standard Strict Baptists.[1]

When Ebenezer Hooper's *Reminiscences of Huntington* was published in 1871 a review from Spurgeon's pen in the *Sword and the Trowel* contained these words:

'A chatty, gossipy book upon one who had, and still has, both ardent friends and fierce detractors. This collection of original anecdotes, letters, and remarks is entirely new, and to some persons will be exceedingly interesting. The compiler is a grandson of three of Huntington's most intimate friends and correspondents; and has thus possessed facilities for gathering up the odds and ends of the renowned Coalheaver's remarkable history. We know the editor and esteem him much . . . On the whole, we do not think so well of Huntington as we did before perusing this highly impartial compilation; he would certainly be a very sad example at home, if the plate-breaking stories are accurate.'

Evidently not all shared Spurgeon's belief in the impartiality of Ebenezer Hooper's account of Huntington for when Hooper produced a second work on the same subject, *Facts, Letters and Documents concerning William*

---

[1] For J. C. Philpot's view of Huntington see *The Gospel Standard,* 1856, pp. 250–60.

*Huntington,* Spurgeon wrote:

'Mr Hooper here continues his honest compilation, nothing extenuating nor setting down aught in malice. He appears to have been savagely assailed for his former work upon the same subject, but we see no ground for it. Few know as much about the celebrated Coalheaver as Mr Hooper does, and fewer still would be as impartial as he has been. Nothing, however, will suit some people but prostration before their idol, and the acceptance of infirmities and mistakes as virtues and inspirations.'[1]

In subsequent discussion of Huntington in the *Sword and the Trowel* Spurgeon defended Huntington from the treatment given to him by E. Paxton Hood:

'We are by no means admirers of all that Huntington preached, wrote, or did; but he ought not to be summarily disposed of as "an amazing piece of spiritual ribaldry" . . . We may be prepared to accept the author's dictum that Huntington's life was "a queer one, a curious compound of romance and ribaldry"; but common honesty requires us to go a good deal further than that, and to believe that at the bottom of what men in their severity call "romance and ribaldry" there was a robust and genuine faith in God . . . There was genius in the Coalheaver of an extraordinary kind, and amazing knowledge of Scripture, a deep experience and a strong faith; and these keep him alive in the hearts of many, despite his bitterness, his Antinomianism, and his arrogance.'[2]

[1] *ST,* 1872, p. 383.
[2] *ST,* 1886, p. 581. These comments followed an initial review of Paxton Hood's book, *The Vocation of the Preacher* on p. 546 of *ST* for the same year.

These words show Spurgeon writing with characteristic fairness. He believed that at opposite extremes, Wesley and Huntington both did 'great good',[1] yet he remained equally convinced that Hyper-Calvinism represented a serious danger to evangelical Christianity. An article in the *Sword and the Trowel* in 1887 argues that conviction in tracing the life of John Stanger, a Baptist pastor who was a contemporary of Huntington's in the south-east of England:

'There was one thing which much saddened Mr Stanger in the later years of his life, and that was the influence of Hyper-Calvinism, which perhaps through the preaching of William Huntington and his imitators, wrought a good deal of mischief in Kent and Sussex. This exaggeration of Calvinism counteracted much that he attempted, and led some away from the simplicity that is in Christ.'[2]

The ill effects of Huntington's influence went a good deal further than the south of England. The biography of Duncan Matheson, the Scottish evangelist who was a frequent correspondent with Spurgeon, contains this passage concerning Matheson's early life as a Christian:

'During this period, in his insatiable hunger for the truth he read incessantly ... In the course of his reading, he stumbled on the writings of Huntington, and for a season was led away into the dreary wilderness of Hyper-Calvinism, where some poor souls seem doomed to wander all their days ... For a time he was bound in the strait jacket of this form of fatalism. He dared not speak to every one of the love of God, lest he should give encouragement to one who was not elect. After a while he discerned

[1] Quoted by Pike, vol. 2, p. 304.
[2] *ST*, 1887, p. 237.

his error, and was led to see that to close the door of the universal call of the gospel is to close the door of salvation against the elect themselves, since the only warrant to believe is simply the general invitation addressed to sinners of mankind.'[1]

Despite the attempted fairness of Spurgeon's words on Huntington, it is not surprising that those who favour 'the Coalheaver' have generally been Spurgeon's strongest critics. He is accorded exactly the same treatment as were Huntington's own evangelical and Calvinistic contemporaries.[2]

[1] *Life and Labours of Duncan Matheson, the Scottish Evangelist*, John MacPherson (London, 1871), p. 47. See also the review in *ST* 1871, p. 286.

[2] Critics of Hyper-Calvinism among Huntington's contemporaries included the evangelical leaders, Rowland Hill and William Jay. When Jay preached Rowland Hill's funeral sermon at the Surrey Chapel, London, in 1833, Wells spoke of the service from his pulpit as 'a big Jay chattering upon a little Hill'. Williams, *Personal Reminiscences,* p. 60.

# 9

## *The Warrant of Faith*
## *– John Brown* [1]

Objection: Are not sinners, as sinners, called to accept and lay hold on Christ in the gospel? and is not he offered to sinners so qualified, and only sinners so and so qualified are called to embrace this offer?

Answer: We cannot say ... that only sinners, so and so qualified by this preparatory work are called, for all are under the gospel that hear the gospel, be they so prepared or not prepared. It is also true, that Christ is offered to sinners as such, that is to such as are living and lying in a state of sin, out of which he must deliver them. But though the deadest sinner, the proudest Pharisee, the greatest justiciary, or self-righteous legalist, is under an obligation

[1] Taken from *A Mirror: or, Looking-Glass for Saint and Sinner* (Glasgow, 1793), pp. 158-9. In the section in which this passage occurs, John Brown (c.1610–79) is dealing with the necessity of the work of the Spirit in conviction of sin, but, as with all the Puritans, he does not confuse this with the warrant upon which the unconverted are called to act. All the Scottish Puritans take the same position as Brown on the warrant of faith. 'God saith to reprobates', writes Rutherford, '"Believe in Christ and ye shall be saved" ' – a truth which he calls 'the deep and special mystery of the Gospel'. *Letters of Samuel Rutherford*, ed. Andrew A. Bonar (1891, repr. Banner of Truth, 1984), p. 468.

to accept of Christ, yet such remaining such, will not accept of Christ and his righteousness, but must first be brought off the false, selfish ground they now stand upon, and quit grips of their own righteousness, ere they be made willing, or be in case to grip Christ, and put him on as their righteousness ...

Objection: Can a soul come too soon to Christ? why then are such preparations, or a preparatory state so spoken of?

Answer: A soul can never too soon come to Christ, if you speak of time: but a soul can too soon think that they are allowed to lay hold on the comforts of Christ, and so deceive themselves. We can give no allowances to hold back any from coming to Christ that are willing; but only hereby shew what is the Lord's ordinary method, and what must precede a soul's closing with Christ, according to the terms of the gospel.

Objection: Is not Christ offered to all freely, that will come to him, and are willing to accept of him? what need then to speak of these preparatory works of the law?

Answer: We grant that Christ is offered freely, and must be taken freely; and what we say of these preparatory works is nothing against the freedom of grace in the gospel; for we look not on these preparatory works as any way meritorious; the Lord's following ordinarily this method with adult persons, does not in the least impair the freedom of the gospel offer; we welcome all that are willing; and if they be but willing to accept of the gospel offer, and will not reject it, we require no more preparation; and this is necessary in all that come to him.

Objection: It would then seem that one is warranted to believe because he is so and so humbled and convinced, not before he has such preparatory works in himself.

I answer, to speak properly, seeing necessity gives not a warrant, but has the force of a strong motive to exert and press the soul to seek help and relief, the call and command of Christ gives the warrant; yet, we say, persons will not lay hold on the call of Christ, nor follow the command, nor come to him upon the warrant of his call, till they see in some measure their necessity, and that otherwise they are undone creatures.

# 10

## *Free-Agency and God's Desire for the Salvation of All – T. J. Crawford*[1]

Thus much, indeed, must in candour be admitted, that we are unable to comprehend *how* an action that was certainly known to God before it was done should, notwithstanding, be free in the performance of it. But then our inability to comprehend *how a thing should come to be,* is no sufficient ground for affirming *that it cannot be.* In the works and ways of God, in the operations of our own minds, and in the processes of our own bodies, there are many things which we know to be actually taking place, without being able fully to account for them, or to reconcile them with other things of the reality of which we are equally well assured. We have no cause to wonder, then, that this should be the case with the divine foreknowledge of human actions on the one hand, and the free agency of man in the performance of them on the other hand. The seeming conflict between them is not *direct,* but *inferential;* and we do not sufficiently comprehend them to be perfectly sure that our inference in regard to their

---

[1] T. J. Crawford (1812–1875) was Professor of Divinity in the University of Edinburgh. The following material is taken from his Baird Lecture for 1874, *The Mysteries of Christianity,* pp. 120–4, 351–2, 356–7.

mutual antagonism is a sound one. The utmost that can be said is, that they appear to be *tending in opposite directions.* But if we knew more about them we might possibly see that, though moving in opposite directions, *they are not moving along the same line,* and hence they cannot come at any time into actual collision.

But, *in the second place,* the contradiction in the case before us not only *may be* but *must be* merely apparent, because we have full and satisfactory evidence that *the two things between which it appears to subsist are both of them true,* and hence that they cannot be really contradictory.

As for our *free agency,* we know it from *our consciousness* – the highest evidence which we can possibly have of any truth. We have the same proof of our free agency that we have of our own existence. And utterly vain is the attempt by metaphysical arguments to reason any sane man out of his conviction of it. Moreover, the whole tenor of the Word of God assumes it – the precepts, warnings, and admonitions of Holy Scripture being all addressed to us on no other footing than that we are the free, voluntary, and responsible originators of our own conduct, which we perfectly well know and feel ourselves to be.

With respect, again, to *God's foreknowledge of human actions,* we have the most profuse and decisive evidence that could be wished. For not to speak of those reasonable grounds on which sound theists have been led to the belief of it, or of those general statements of Holy Scripture in which it is broadly and articulately affirmed, we can point to a vast assemblage of prophecies relating to the conduct of moral and accountable agents, in which the divine prescience[1] is actually exemplified. Notably we can point to

[1] i.e., foreknowledge.

the predictions relative to the conduct of our Lord's enemies when they crucified Him; for of *them* – not the less that they are charged as responsible agents with the awful crime of having slain with wicked hands the Lord of glory – it is expressly said that 'they did to Him whatsoever things the hand and counsel of God had before determined to be done.'

Here, then, we have *two truths* – (1) that man is a free agent, and (2) that his actions were foreknown by the omniscient God – each supported by evidence that is suited to the nature of it, and calculated to produce a full and unwavering belief. And mark *this,* moreover – *there is no conflict between the evidences of them,* whatever there may seem to be between the truths which these evidences substantiate. The proofs of our free agency do not in any way invalidate or even touch the proofs of the divine prescience; and as little, on the other hand, do the proofs of the divine prescience invalidate or even touch the proofs of our free agency. If we look, then, at each of these truths by itself, and candidly weigh its evidence, we have no alternative but to believe it. And if we believe *each* on its own proper and sufficient grounds, then must we believe *both,* unable though we may be to perceive their connection or harmony with one another. Nay, more. If we believe both of these things to be true, there is one thing more that we must needs believe concerning them, and that is, that they are consistent or compatible, and that any appearance of their being otherwise must be fallacious. For it is unquestionable that anything that is true must necessarily be consistent with every other thing that is true. *We,* indeed, may not be able to see their consistency, but we may be very sure that *God sees it.* And we also should see it if we had the same perfect knowledge which He possesses of the whole assemblage of truths in all their relations and dependencies.

\* \* \*

It may be alleged, however, that the invitations of the Gospel, besides being expressive of the undisputed fact that whosoever complies with them shall obtain the offered blessings, are also indicative of *a desire on the part of God that all sinners to whom they are held out should comply with them;* and how, it may be asked, can such a *desire* be sincere, if it be the *purpose of God to confer only on some sinners* that grace by which their compliance will be secured?

Now, without pretending that we are able to give a satisfactory answer to this question, we are not prepared to admit, what the question evidently assumes, that God can have no sincere *desire* with reference to the conduct of all His creatures, if it be His *purpose* to secure on the part of some, and not on the part of all of them, the fulfilment of this desire. For how does the case stand in this respect with His *commandments?* These, no less than His invitations, are addressed to all. Both are alike to be considered as indications of what He desires and requires to be done by all. Nor are there wanting, with reference to His commandments, testimonies quite as significant as any which are to be found with reference to His invitations, of the earnestness and intensity of His desire that the course which they prescribe should be adopted by all who hear them. Take, for example, these tender expostulations: 'O that there were such a heart in them, that they would fear me, and keep all my commandments always, that it might be well with them, and with their children for ever!' 'Oh that my people had hearkened unto me, and Israel had walked in my ways!' 'O that thou hadst hearkened to my commandments; then had thy peace been as a river, and thy righteousness as the waves of the sea!'

But while the commandments of God are thus indicative of what God *desires, approves of,* and *delights in,* as congenial to the goodness and holiness of His moral nature, they are certainly not declarative, at the same time, of what He has fixedly *purposed or determined in His government of the universe to carry into effect.* For if they were so, it is certain that they would be unfailingly and universally obeyed by all His creatures; whereas they are frequently violated, without any interference on His part to secure their observance. Doubtless it is an inscrutable mystery that things should thus be done under the government of the Almighty which are in the highest degree displeasing and offensive to Him. It is just the old mystery of the existence of moral evil, which no one has ever been able to explain.

\*　　\*　　\*

Finally, however unable we may be to reconcile the calls and invitations addressed to all sinners with God's purpose of electing grace, we may be assured that *to the eye of God they are reconcilable* like many other things in His unsearchable works and ways which seem to our limited minds to be equally mysterious. For our part, we find ourselves necessitated *to believe both the one and the other* (although we cannot discern on what principle they are to be harmonised) on the clear Scriptural grounds that may severally be assigned for them. We do well to be exceedingly diffident in our judgments respecting matters so unsearchable as the secret purposes of God. Whatever the Scriptures may have *expressly affirmed* regarding the fact *that God has such purposes,* we are bound in a humble and teachable spirit to believe. But when we proceed to *draw inferences* from such affirmations, to the effect of weakening our confidence in other statements – emanating from the same source and equally explicit – with reference to things that are more level to our comprehension, we are certainly going beyond our proper province. And therefore, convinced though we be, on the authority of Scripture, that it is God's purpose to bring an elect people to a willing and hearty reception of the great salvation, we cannot, and never will, thence deduce any conclusions tending to obscure the brightness of that manifestation which God has made of His love to a sinful world in the mediatorial work and sufferings of His beloved Son, or to cast a shadow of doubt on the earnestness of His desire, as indicated in the calls and offers of the Gospel, that all sinners should come to the Saviour that they may have life.

## 11

# *A Crucial Text – C. H. Spurgeon on 1 Timothy 2:3, 4* [1]

*'God our Saviour, who will have all men to be saved, and to come unto the knowledge of the truth.'*

May God the Holy Ghost guide our meditations to the best practical result this evening, that sinners may be saved and saints stirred up to diligence.

I do not intend to treat my text controversially. It is like the stone which makes the corner of a building, and it looks towards a different side of the gospel from that which is mostly before us. Two sides of the building of truth meet here. In many a village there is a corner where the idle and the quarrelsome gather together; and theology has such corners. It would be very easy indeed to set ourselves in battle array, and during the next half-hour to carry on a very fierce attack against those who differ from us in opinion upon points which could be raised from this text. I do not see that any good would come of it, and, as we have very little time to spare, and life is short, we had better

[1] This provides an excellent summary of Spurgeon's thought on one of the principal issues relating to the Hyper-Calvinistic controversy. It is taken from the opening words of a sermon published in *MTP*, vol. 26, pp. 49–52.

spend it upon something that may better tend to our edification. May the good Spirit preserve us from a contentious spirit, and help us really to profit by his word.

It is quite certain that when we read that God will have all men to be saved it does not mean that he wills it with the force of a decree or a divine purpose, for, if he did, then all men would be saved. He willed to make the world, and the world was made: he does not so will the salvation of all men, for we know that all men will not be saved. Terrible as the truth is, yet is it certain from holy writ that there are men who, in consequence of their sin and their rejection of the Saviour, will go away into everlasting punishment, where shall be weeping and wailing and gnashing of teeth. There will at the last be goats upon the left hand as well as sheep on the right, tares to be burned as well as wheat to be garnered, chaff to be blown away as well as corn to be preserved. There will be a dreadful hell as well as a glorious heaven, and there is no decree to the contrary.

What then? Shall we try to put another meaning into the text than that which it fairly bears? I trow not. You must, most of you, be acquainted with the general method in which our older Calvinistic friends deal with this text. 'All men,' say they, – 'that is, *some men*': as if the Holy Ghost could not have said 'some men' if he had meant some men. 'All men,' say they; 'that is, some of all sorts of men': as if the Lord could not have said 'All sorts of men' if he had meant that. The Holy Ghost by the apostle has written 'all men,' and unquestionably he means all men. I know how to get rid of the force of the 'alls' according to that critical method which some time ago was very current, but I do not see how it can be applied here with due regard to truth. I was reading just now the exposition of a very able doctor who explains the text so as to explain it away; he applies grammatical gunpowder to it, and explodes it by way of expounding it. I thought when I read his exposition that it would have been a very capital comment upon the text if it had read, 'Who *will not* have all men to be saved, nor come to a knowledge of the truth.' Had such been the inspired language every remark of the learned doctor would have been exactly in keeping, but as it happens to say, 'Who *will* have all men to be saved,' his observations are more than a little out of place. My love of consistency with my own doctrinal views is not great enough to allow me knowingly to alter a single text of Scripture. I have great respect for orthodoxy, but my reverence for inspiration is far greater. I would sooner a hundred times over appear to be inconsistent with myself than be inconsistent with the word of God. I never thought it to be any very great crime to seem to be inconsistent with myself, for who am I that I should everlastingly be consistent? But I do think it a great crime to be so inconsistent with the word of God that I should want to lop away a bough or even a twig from so much as a single tree of the forest of Scripture. God forbid that I should cut or shape, even in the least degree, any divine expression. So runs the text, and so we must read it, 'God our Saviour; who will have all men to be saved, and to come unto the knowledge of the truth.'

Does not the text mean that it is the wish of God that men should be saved? The word 'wish' gives as much force to the original as it really requires, and the passage should run thus – 'whose wish it is that all men should be saved and come to a knowledge of the truth.' As it is *my* wish that it should be so, as it is *your* wish that it might be so, so it is God's wish that all men should be saved; for, assuredly, he is not less benevolent than we are. Then comes the question, 'But if he wishes it to be so, why does he not make it so?' Beloved friend, have you never heard that a fool may ask a question which a wise man cannot answer, and, if that be so, I am sure a wise person, like yourself, can ask me a great many questions which, fool as I am, I am yet not foolish enough to try to answer. Your question is only one form of the great debate of all the ages, – 'If God be infinitely good and powerful, why does not his power carry out to the full all his beneficence?' It is God's wish that the oppressed should go free, yet there are many oppressed who are not free. It is God's wish that the sick should not suffer. Do you doubt it? Is it not your own wish? And yet the Lord does not work a miracle to heal every sick person. It is God's wish that his creatures should be happy. Do you deny that? He does not interpose by any miraculous agency to make us all happy, and yet it would be wicked to suppose that he does not wish the happiness of all the creatures that he has made. He has an infinite benevolence which, nevertheless, is not in all points worked out by his infinite omnipotence; and if anybody asked me why it is not, I cannot tell. I have never set up to be an explainer of all difficulties, and I have no desire to do so. It is the same old question as that of the negro who said, 'Sare, you say the devil makes sin in the world.' 'Yes, the devil makes a deal of sin.' 'And you say that God hates sin.' 'Yes.' 'Then why does not he kill the devil and put an end to it?' Just so. Why does he not? Ah, my black friend, you will grow white before that question is answered. I cannot tell you why God permits moral evil, neither can the ablest philosopher on earth, nor the highest angel in heaven.

This is one of those things which we do not need to

know. Have you never noticed that some people who are ill and are ordered to take pills are foolish enough to chew them? That is a very nauseous thing to do, though I have done it myself. The right way to take medicine of such a kind is to swallow it at once. In the same way there are some things in the Word of God which are undoubtedly true which must be swallowed at once by an effort of faith, and must not be chewed by perpetual questioning. You will soon have I know not what of doubt and difficulty and bitterness upon your soul if you must needs know the unknowable, and have reasons and explanations for the sublime and the mysterious. Let the difficult doctrines go down whole into your very soul, by a grand exercise of confidence in God.

I thank God for a thousand things I cannot understand. When I cannot get to know the reason why, I say to myself, 'Why should I know the reason why? Who am I, and what am I, that I should demand explanations of my God?' I am a most unreasonable being when I am most reasonable, and when my judgment is most accurate I dare not trust it. I had rather trust my God. I am a poor silly child at my very best: but my Father must know better than I. An old parable-maker tells us that he shut himself up in his study because he had to work out a difficult problem. His little child came knocking at the door, and he said 'Go away, John: you cannot understand what father is doing: let father alone.' Master Johnny for that very reason felt that he must get in and see what father was doing – a true symbol of our proud intellects; we must pry into forbidden things, and uncover that which is concealed. In a little time upon the sill, outside the window, stood Master Johnny, looking in through the window at his father; and if his father had not with the very tenderest care just taken him away from that very dangerous position, there would have been no Master Johnny left on the face of the earth to exercise his curiosity in dangerous elevations. Now, God sometimes shuts the door, and says, 'My child, it is so: be content to believe.' 'But,' we foolishly cry, 'Lord, why is it so?' 'It is so, my child,' he says. 'But why, Father, is it so?' 'It is so, my child, believe me.' Then we go on speculating, climbing the ladders of reasoning, guessing, speculating, to reach the lofty windows of eternal truth. Once up there we do not know where we are, our heads reel, and we are in all kinds of uncertainty and spiritual peril. If we mind things too high for us we shall run great risks. I do not intend meddling with such lofty matters. There stands the text, and I believe that it is my Father's wish that 'all men should be saved, and come to the knowledge of the truth.' But I know, also, that he does not will it, so that he will save any one of them, unless they believe in his dear Son; for he has told us over and over that he will not. He will not save any man except he forsakes his sins, and turns to him with full purpose of heart: that I also know. And I know, also, that he has a people whom he will save, whom by his eternal love he has chosen, and whom by his eternal power he will deliver. I do not know how that squares with this; that is another of the things I do not know. If I go on telling you of all that I do not know, and of all that I do know, I will warrant you that the things that I do not know will be a hundred to one of the things that I do know. And so we will say no more about the matter, but just go on to the more practical part of the text. God's wish about man's salvation is this, – that men should be saved and come to the knowledge of the truth.

## 12

## *The Injury Done by Hyper-Calvinism and Antinomianism – Words of Witness from Spurgeon*[1]

The true minister of Christ feels impelled to preach the whole truth, because it and it alone can meet the wants of man. What evils has this world seen through a distorted, mangled, man-moulded gospel.

What mischiefs have been done to the souls of men by men who have preached only one part and not all the counsel of God! My heart bleeds for many a family where Antinomian doctrine has gained the sway. I could tell many a sad story of families dead in sin, whose consciences are seared as with a hot iron, by the fatal preaching to which they listen. I have known convictions stifled and desires quenched by the soul-destroying system which takes manhood from man and makes him no more responsible than an ox. I cannot imagine a more ready instrument in the hands of Satan for the ruin of souls than a minister who tells sinners that it is not their duty to repent of their sins or to believe in Christ, and who has the arrogance to call himself a gospel minister, while he teaches that God hates some men infinitely and unchangeably for no reason whatever

---

[1] Taken from a sermon preached 11 December 1859. *NPSP*, vol. 6, pp. 28–9.

but simply because he chooses to do so.[1] O my brethren! may the Lord save you from the voice of the charmer, and keep you ever deaf to the voice of error.

Even in Christian families, what evil will a distorted gospel produce! I have seen the young believer, just saved from sin, happy in his early Christian career, and walking humbly with his God. But evil has crept in, disguised in the mantle of truth. The finger of partial blindness was laid upon their eyes, and but one doctrine could be seen. Sovereignty was seen, but not responsibility. The minister once beloved was hated; he who had been honest to preach God's Word, was accounted as the off-scouring of all things. And what became the effect? The very reverse of good and gracious. Bigotry usurped the place of love; bitterness lived where once there had been a loveliness of character. I could point you to innumerable instances where harping upon any one peculiar doctrine has driven men to excess of bigotry and bitterness. And when a man has once come there, he is ready enough for sin of any kind to which the devil may please to tempt him. There is a necessity that the whole gospel should be preached, or else the spirits, even of Christians, will become marred and maimed. I have known men diligent for Christ, labouring to win souls with both hands; and on a sudden they have espoused one particular doctrine and not the whole truth, and they have subsided into lethargy. On the other hand, where men have only taken the practical side of truth, and left out the doctrinal, too many professors have run over into legality; have talked as if they were to be saved by

[1] A reference to Wells' letters on sovereignty then appearing in the *Earthen Vessel*, see above, p. 62.

works, and have almost forgotten that grace by which they were called. They are like the Galatians; they have been bewitched by what they have heard. The believer in Christ, if he is to be kept pure, simple, holy, charitable, Christ-like, is only to be kept so by a preaching of the whole truth as it is in Jesus. And as for the salvation of sinners, ah, my hearers, we can never expect God to bless our ministry for the conversion of sinners unless we preach the gospel as a whole. Let me get but one part of the truth, and always dwell upon it, to the exclusion of every other, and I cannot expect my Master's blessing. If I preach as he would have me preach, he will certainly own the word; he will never leave it without his own living witness. But let me imagine that I can improve the gospel, that I can make it consistent, that I can dress it up and make it look finer, I shall find that my Master is departed, and that Ichabod is written on the walls of the sanctuary. How many there are kept in bondage through neglect of gospel invitations.

## A DIAGRAM OF ENGLISH BAPTIST HISTORY

For the general guidance of readers unfamiliar with this field, Dr Robert Oliver has kindly provided the outline on the following page. It should be realized, however, that a diagram necessarily represents a simplification and that history contains many nuances which cannot be conveyed in this way. The main heavy line in the diagram shows where the numerical preponderance lay. Initially all churches on this line were 'Particular' (i.e., holding to the Calvinistic position on the extent of the atonement) and many were also 'strict', which is to say, they required immersion of all received at the Lord's Table. Others allowed 'open communion'. Both 'strict' and 'open' churches remained in fellowship until the late eighteenth and early nineteenth centuries when there were prolonged controversies over law, faith and terms of communion. At that time, through the influence of William Gadsby, John Stevens and others, those churches which were both Calvinistic and opposed to open communion began to move apart under the designation of 'Strict and Particular Baptist', subsequently sub-dividing in their affiliation in terms of the particular magazine with which they often came to be identified. Most of these changes were gradual, rather than occurring at specific dates, and so much overlap continued to exist that the Religious Census of 1851 continued to group all 'Particular Baptists' together, whether 'Strict' or not. During the nineteenth century the Strict and Particular Baptists commonly favoured Hyper-Calvinism while others in the Particular Baptist line gradually moved towards Arminianism, making possible the Union of 1891.

For further detail see Dr Oliver's unpublished Ph.D. thesis (1986), 'The Emergence of a Strict and Particular Baptist Community Among the English Calvinistic Baptists, 1770–1850', deposited in the British Library and available on microfiche through Inter-Library loan.

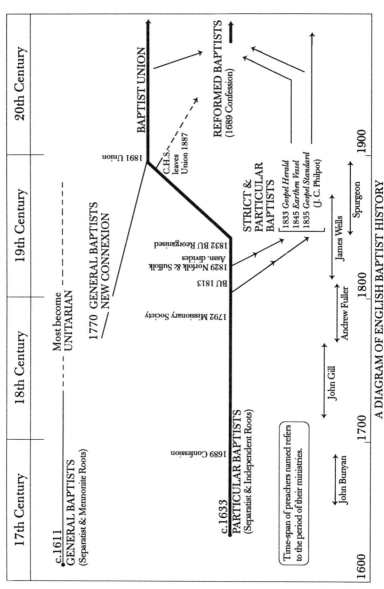

A DIAGRAM OF ENGLISH BAPTIST HISTORY

| 17th Century | 18th Century | 19th Century | 20th Century |

c.1611
GENERAL BAPTISTS
(Separatist & Mennonite Roots)

Most become UNITARIAN

1770 GENERAL BAPTISTS NEW CONNEXION

BAPTIST UNION

1891 Union

C.H.S. leaves Union 1887

REFORMED BAPTISTS
(1689 Confession)

1832 BU Reorganised

1829 Norfolk & Suffolk Assn. divides

BU 1813

1792 Missionary Society

STRICT & PARTICULAR BAPTISTS

[1833 *Gospel Herald*
1845 *Earthen Vessel*
1835 *Gospel Standard* (J. C. Philpot)]

c.1633
PARTICULAR BAPTISTS
(Separatist & Independent Roots)

1689 Confession

John Bunyan

John Gill

Andrew Fuller

James Wells

Spurgeon

Time-span of preachers named refers to the period of their ministries.

1600      1700      1800      1900

[159]

## SPURGEON TITLES CURRENTLY PUBLISHED
## BY THE BANNER OF TRUTH TRUST

*Advice to Seekers*

*An All-Round Ministry, Addresses to Ministers and Students*

*Commenting and Commentaries,* Two lectures, a catalogue and full textual index to his sermons.

*The Forgotten Spurgeon,* Iain H. Murray

*Letters of C. H. Spurgeon,* ed. Iain H. Murray

*Life and Work of Charles Haddon Spurgeon,* G. Holden Pike, 6 vols. bound in 2.

*Metropolitan Tabernacle Pulpit*:
   Vol. 38 for the year 1892.

*Revival Year Sermons, Preached in the Surrey Music Hall*

*Spurgeon Autobiography:*
   Vol. 1: *The Early Years* *
   Vol. 2: *The Full Harvest* *

*Spurgeon, A New Biography,* Arnold Dallimore

*Newcomers to Spurgeon are recommended to begin with the titles marked by an asterisk.

# Index

# EVANGELICALISM DIVIDED:
## A RECORD OF CRUCIAL CHANGE
## IN THE YEARS 1950 - 2000

ISBN 0 85151 783 8

352 pp., cloth-bound

'The book is a page turner from first to last . . . It left me asking, "Has the last fifty years seen evangelicals broaden the road to the extent that the Christian message is compromised and uncertain?"'

Peter Breckwoldt, *Church of England Newspaper*

'Murray's critique is as kind as it is revealing and devastating. The icons of modern evangelism are shown as falling into egregious strategic errors which have weakened the evangelical faith at its very core. The bridges built to reach the mainstream became a two-way street by which those who sought to influence the liberals were themselves influenced.'

R. C. Sproul, *Table Talk*

'Murray presents a convincing argument with cogent evidence. His ability to concentrate on the bigger picture, without ignoring necessary details, ensures that he takes the reader with him. There is no doubt that there will be readers of this book who will take exception to some of his conclusions, but the broad thesis stands firm. This book is probably one of the most important church history books published in 2000 and every church leader ought to read it.'

Brian Talbot, *Scottish Baptist Website*

## D. MARTYN LLOYD-JONES:
## THE FIRST FORTY YEARS, 1899–1939
### (Volume 1 of the Authorized Biography)

ISBN 0 85151 353 0

412 pp., cloth-bound, illustrated

'Certain to be one of the major biographies of any Christian leader of the twentieth century.'

*Sword and Trowel* (Australia)

'If Martyn Lloyd-Jones' life were a novel it would be panned by critics as too unrealistic. Because his life is a historical reality we are left to wonder at the providential energy that could have effected such an astonishing career . . . This book is an electrifying apologetic for the powerfully theologized pulpit emphases of the Reformers and Puritans. Such an approach was in eclipse when Lloyd-Jones began his ministry. The renaissance of interest in Reformed theology is due in no small way to this man; he himself would attribute the resurgence to the sovereign grace of God.'

*Christianity Today*

'All credit to Iain Murray for clothing the bare bones of the story with a fascinating store of anecdote about the man and his ministry. For preachers and ministers especially, this is a biography to be savoured and pondered, as well as to be revelled in.'

*Floodtide*

# D. MARTYN LLOYD-JONES:
## THE FIGHT OF FAITH, 1939-1981
### (Volume 2 of the Authorized Biography)

ISBN 0 85151 564 9
862 pp., cloth-bound, illustrated

'This long awaited work is a worthy conclusion to the first volume published in 1982 . . . The life of Martyn Lloyd-Jones, much more than the story of one man's life, is really the story of evangelicalism in general and modern British evangelicalism in particular. Often Lloyd-Jones was the lone foil to many popular tendencies in evangelicalism . . . This biography should be added to the God-called pastor's reading if he wants to understand the times and receive benefit from the life of a man who will probably be viewed in the years ahead as our century's most enduring and doctrinally strong pastoral preacher.'

John Armstrong, *Trinity Journal*

'Splendidly written and passes the litmus test as a good and absorbing read from a biographer completely at home and in tune with his subject.'

*Methodist Recorder*

'Highly recommended, especially for those hungry for "iron rations".'

*Christian Renewal* (Canada)

JONATHAN EDWARDS:
A NEW BIOGRAPHY

ISBN 0 85151 704 8
536 pp., paperback, illustrated

'This is my book of the year for which I have waited a lifetime.'
Graham Miller, *Australian Presbyterian Life*

'Surely Murray's fine biography will gain the audience it deserves.'
*William and Mary Quarterly*

'A biography giving proper weight to the spiritual life and stature of Jonathan Edwards was needed . . . This is what Iain Murray has provided and he has done the job well. He has unique skill in this area.'
J. I. Packer, Vancouver

'Murray provides a standard of excellence among Christian biographers. Edwards' life, especially as he presents it, offers significant challenge to Christians. No one should come away from it without being challenged to a deeper commitment to Jesus Christ, a greater desire for prayer and wholeheartedness, and a stronger resolve to be a doer of the Word as well as a hearer.'
*Moody Monthly*

## REVIVAL AND REVIVALISM:
## THE MAKING AND MARRING OF AMERICAN
## EVANGELICALISM, 1750-1858

ISBN 0 85151 660 2
480 pp., cloth-bound, illustrated

'It is a rare book that hits both head and heart in a way that turns a life. *Revival and Revivalism* had that effect on me, providing a clear and convincing perspective on the role and importance of revivals in American church history, bringing me to a new stage in my spiritual pilgrimage, and giving me a new hope for the prospects of the gospel in the world.'

Scott McCullough, *Blue Banner* (Pittsburgh)

'Murray has uncovered much fresh information which, I suspect, will surprise and delight even the most seasoned reader . . . a valuable new resource.'

Garth M. Rosell, *American Presbyterians*

'Murray's main point is also theologically compelling: when religion becomes something that humans work up for God (i.e. "revivalism") instead of something God graciously bestows upon repentant sinners (i.e. "revival"), the integrity of the faith is at stake .'

Mark A. Noll, *Christianity Today*

'A remarkably stimulating and helpful book.'

D. Clair Davis, *Evangelicals Now*

# THE FORGOTTEN SPURGEON

ISBN 0 85151 156 2

256 pp., paperback, illustrated

'Iain Murray has written a fascinating book. It should not be read once, but several times, and in addition, certain passages should frequently be meditated upon. It is not a biography of Spurgeon, but it is a study (written in an interesting and absorbing style) of three of the doctrinal controversies through which Spurgeon had to go. To read this book will bring us face to face with some solemn questions. Cannot we abandon some of the frivolities in which we engage, and pray for a revival of preaching? Is it not time that we stop being concerned about *communicating* the gospel and become concerned about *preaching* it?'

Edward J. Young, Westminster Theological Seminary

'Iain Murray has done us a great service in providing this interpretive account of the influence and testimony of C. H. Spurgeon. Not only has he sought to evaluate Spurgeon's significance in his own day ... He has examined the contribution of Spurgeon's ministry in the context of the whole history of Evangelical Protestantism. The book deserves a wide reading because it deals not with 'The Forgotten Spurgeon' alone, but also with the forgotten gospel.'

*The Evangelical Magazine*

THE PURITAN HOPE
Revival and the
Interpretation of Prophecy

ISBN 0 85151 247 X
328 pp., paperback, illustrated

'In the present sad state of the Christian church this book should prove to be a tonic. It is different from the vague and loosely conceived remedies derived from human wisdom offered to relierve the modern distress. Iain Murray urges the believing church to lay hold of the theology of the Puritans and engage in its hearty and forthright proclamation as the only means to stop the retreat from Christianity. '

*Westminster Theological Journal*

'Mr Murray has written a book of high importance which deserves to be studied and pondered by evangelical Christians. How can readiness for Christ's Coming be consistent with the belief that revivals are yet to be given to the church? Questions such as this are brought to the fore in this book, and the author, employing both exposition of Scripture and much historical and biographical material, sets out the case for believing that it is not orthodox to indulge in gloom over the prospects for Christianity in the world.'

*Dedication*

PENTECOST – TODAY?
The Biblical Basis for
Understanding Revival

ISBN 0 85151 752 8
234 pp., cloth-bound

'Many Christians are excited about the prospect of revival but little attention has been given to understanding its biblical basis . . . In this context Iain Murray's book must be welcomed . . . This is a hugely interesting work and one which is a necessary corrective to the superficial views and empty claims of much modern revivalism. Its grasp of theology and of history would enrich anyone's understanding of revival and all concerned with the issue ought to engage with what he has written.'

*Theological Book Review*

'Although I differ from the author at a number of points in his theology of the Holy Spirit, I hope profoundly that this new book is read by many of my fellow charismatics, for there is much wisdom and depth here that is badly needed in the circles I now move in . . . If you are a church leader you owe it to your people to read this sober assessment of where we are today, whatever your theological position.'

*CLC Reviews of Books*

*For free illustrated catalogue please write to:*
THE BANNER OF TRUTH TRUST
*3 Murrayfield Road, Edinburgh EH12 6EL, U.K., or
P. O. Box 621, Carlisle, Pennsylvania 17013, U.S.A.*